Thrill Me

Also by BENJAMIN PERCY

The Dead Lands
Red Moon
The Wilding
Refresh, Refresh
The Language of Elk

Thrill Me

ESSAYS ON FICTION

BENJAMIN PERCY

Graywolf Press

This publication is made possible, in part, by the voters of Minnesota through a Minnesota State Arts Board Operating Support grant, thanks to a legislative appropriation from the arts and cultural heritage fund, and through a grant from the Wells Fargo Foundation Minnesota. Significant support has also been provided by Target, the McKnight Foundation, the Amazon Literary Partnership, and other generous contributions from foundations, corporations, and individuals. To these organizations and individuals we offer our heartfelt thanks.

Published by Graywolf Press
250 Third Avenue North, Suite 600
Minneapolis, Minnesota 55401

www.graywolfpress.org

Published in the United States of America

ISBN 978-1-55597-759-7

2 4 6 8 9 7 5 3 1
First Graywolf Printing, 2016

Library of Congress Control Number: 2016931536

Cover design: Kyle G. Hunter

Cover art: CSA Images / Color Printstock Collection / Getty Images

For
Trish King, Carol O'Shea, Theresa Wadden,
Ben Marcus, Meredith Steinbach,
Robert Arellano, Beth Lordan,
Brady Udall, and Mike Magnuson,
the teachers who lit the way.

Contents

Thrill Me

Thrill Me

Vampires, dragons, and robots with laser eyes. These were the literary stars of my childhood. Their stories were unified by the same pattern: they began with a bang—high jinks ensued and then the hero overcame some villainous force to win love and a heap of treasure. Books were portals meant for escapism. Suck me into the tornado, beam me through an intergalactic transporter, drag me down the rabbit hole, and then, please, quicken my pulse for the next three hundred to seven hundred pages.

I had no patience for anything that did not meet these criteria. This narrow-mindedness extended to any creative discipline. In college, I took a class called A History of Art and Architecture, and during the lecture on Jackson Pollock, I was fool enough to throw up my hand and ask how a bunch of splatter could be considered art. "Who's it about? Where's the story?" I said in an auditorium of several hundred students. "What distinguishes that from garbage?" At that moment I think every single one of them muttered under their breath that I was an idiot. The professor smiled at me sadly and thanked me for my opinion before changing the slide and continuing her lecture. This is one of those memories that, years later, still haunts me at odd times—when I'm driving along a nighttime highway or soaping my armpits in the shower—and I cringe as if I had just bitten into tinfoil.

I did not fare much better in my creative writing workshop. On the first day, the professor reviewed the syllabus, listing off due dates, required readings, and finally announcing that there would be no genre submissions. Then he asked if we had any questions. His shaved head and expressionless face made him look a little like a mannequin.

"What do you mean by no genre?" I said.

He leveled his dead gaze at me and said, "I mean no genre. No vampires, no dragons, no robots with laser eyes. Do you understand?" He took off his glasses and scanned the room. "Does everyone understand?"

I didn't. With complete earnestness I asked, "But what else *is* there?" and in response he gave me the same pitying smile my art professor had.

When people ask if I grew up a reader, I say yes, but not the type of reader they imagine: a small, scholarly child with glasses perched on the end of his nose, making notes in a leather-bound journal, licking the pad of his finger to turn the pages of *Ulysses, The Grapes of Wrath, To the Lighthouse.* I grew up on pop lit. A book was never far from my hand—balanced on my nightstand, shoved into a back pocket, tucked into the glove compartment of the truck—but usually it was a broken-spined mass-market paperback with an embossed title.

I lived on twenty-seven acres of woods in the Willamette Valley— and then a jungly hillside in Oahu overlooking Kaneohe Bay—and then a spread of land in central Oregon surrounded by sage flats and horse ranches. Always the country. I didn't play sports, not until middle school, and I didn't have any neighborhood pals.

Okay, there were the Marshalls. Many people in central Oregon grow alfalfa for cattle, but the Marshalls cultivated, on their five acres, perfectly manicured grass. Not to sell and not to play on. The grass seemed to exist purely to mow and water. Their mother answered the phone "Heaven-O!" (because she didn't like saying *hell*).

A birthday party consisted of a living room piano recital and Bible reading followed by Fudgsicles. By the time I was in sixth grade—after I had exposed them to the "black magic" of the film *Big Trouble in Little China* and gotten busted for smoking cigarettes and shooting rocks at cars with my slingshot—they were forbidden from playing with me. So I was on my own. And after completing my father's list of chores for the day, I was able to spend my time as I wished. I would duck under barbed-wire fences, build rock dams in rivers, knock together tree houses with wood stolen from construction sites, and read.

And I read a lot. A book or two a week. Westerns by Zane Grey and Louis L'Amour. Spy thrillers by John le Carré and Ian Fleming. Techno thrillers by Tom Clancy. Mysteries by Sir Arthur Conan Doyle and Tony Hillerman. For a long time, fantasy obsessed me. If it had a dragon on the cover, awesome. If it had a dragon and a sword, even better. I delighted in *The Hobbit* and *The Lord of the Rings,* of course, but so did I read The Wheel of Time series and *Dragons of Autumn Twilight* and all the Forgotten Realms novels about Dritz, the dark elf who wielded twin scimitars and traveled with a black panther. I pleasured as much in the sword and sorcery of Conan novels as I did in their covers, all of them featuring some variation on the impossibly muscular Cimmerian strangling a demon with one hand and clutching a woman with the other, her nakedness barely contained by wisps of silk, chains of silver.

But horror, more than any other genre, caught me repeatedly in its black spiderweb. I'm talking about Peter Straub, Richard Matheson, Dean Koontz, Anne Rice, Robert R. McCammon, Shirley Jackson, John Saul, Dan Simmons, and Stephen King. Their hundreds of thousands of pages I read in a panic. You know how certain settings sizzle with a kind of electricity? Old churches. Graveyards. The elbow of a river. The top of a mountain. For me, the horror section in Powell's Books is sacred ground.

My grandparents lived in Portland, Oregon, so every few months,

we'd cram into the truck and growl over the mountains for a visit.
We had no local bookstore—outside of the sad little Waldenbooks
in the Bend River Mall—so the Powell's visit took a lot of time and
strategy. This was our literary haul for the next two months. We had
to choose wisely.

For those who have never visited it, the downtown Powell's takes
up a whole city block. A giant concrete split-level sarcophagus of
books. There is a ghost that haunts the water fountain. An urn of
cremated remains that moves from room to room. The shelves spill
books, used and new, and the aisles buzz with the kind of diversity
you'll only find at the DMV: dudes in suits and dudes in mud-caked
cowboy boots, a woman with dreads and a woman with a tiara and
a woman with bright blue hair. A carnival of wonders for a kid from
the boonies.

We would push our way through the Tenth and Burnside doors,
and the smell of paper and ink and glue (and oftentimes patchouli)
would result in a sensory overload. I would feel jittery and starved.
I would cut through the Blue Room (which I loved, too, but always
thought of as English class, home to all of the *serious* lit-a-ra-ture)
and slowly, slowly make my way through the Gold Room, home to
all the sci-fi and fantasy and thrillers and horror novels.

The smell there—sort of mildewy earthworm meets mottled
paper—is one of my favorite smells. The horror aisle is shadow-
soaked, far from any window. Over the next few hours I would pull
down books and read them cross-legged on the floor and build a
dark tower of paperbacks, the greatest treasure of my childhood.

I remember the first moment terror enchanted me. I was a kinder-
gartner at Crow Elementary School, and in the library one day I
pulled off the shelf the book *Universal Studios Monsters*. I flipped
through its pages, studying the stills from *Frankenstein, Dracula,
The Mummy, The Wolf Man*. I lingered on the image of Lon Chaney
Jr., with his fanged underbite, his hoggish nose and shag-carpeting
hair, so long that it burned into my memory and haunted me later

that night, when I cried out for my parents and could fall asleep only trembling between them. I knew terror—but I also knew the spike of adrenaline that comes with it. The very next day at school I returned to that same corner of the library and cracked the book again, an addict seeking another hit.

I read novels for the same kind of thrill—to escape, to supplement the boredom of one life with the excitement and dagger-sharp danger of another. Sometimes the worlds merged. I would crawl through a drainpipe and imagine myself one of the children in Stephen King's *It*. I would place a pencil on my desk and bring my fingers to my temples and focus for an hour, trying to move it with my mind, trying to channel the telekinetic powers of Carrie. I once stayed up all night—with my sheet wrapped elaborately around me like a cotton shield, a porthole for my mouth the only part of me exposed—because I was convinced the shadowy mass in the corner of my room was the creature from Dean Koontz's *Watchers*.

This is why I treated the Marshalls less as people and more as characters in a horror story I was building. Because I wanted to keep living the nightmare. The Marshalls were innocents. They could listen to U2—and no other contemporary rock—because of its Christian themes. They were forbidden to play Ghost in the Graveyard—a game of tag played at night with flashlights—unless we renamed it Baby in the Carriage. So I made a hobby out of ruining them. I told them a shadow-man, no doubt a demon, lived in our chicken coop. I taught them every swear word I knew. I read them the pinkest, sweatiest sex passages from *The Clan of the Cave Bear*. I dared them to smoke cigarettes, to drink the soda and eat the candy they weren't allowed—and then I wondered aloud what their parents would think if they discovered their wrongdoing. I was painfully bored, obviously twisted, and already practicing, I now realize, for a life as a writer. I identified the flaws, the weaknesses of my characters—and exploited them—like a thumb digging into the rotten spot of an apple.

I'm sorry to say that my sister suffered terribly. I would toss spiders into her hair, leap out of closets with my hands made into claws. I would shut off the lights when she was in the bathroom. I would creep up behind her in a demon mask and tap her on the shoulder and when she twisted around she would scream and then laugh and then hit me.

She had a collection of troll dolls. The ones with the bug eyes and the wild hair. And I would move them around, sneaking one under her pillow, another into her sock drawer, another into the cereal box so that it would tumble into her bowl, and when she asked if I did it, I would give her a dead-faced look and say, "What are you talking about?" One time I snuck into her room late at night and rearranged the troll dolls, all twenty of them, into a line next to her bed. When she awoke the next morning she found them staring at her, one of them carrying a note that read, "BAD DREAMS," with the R and the S backward (for trollish authenticity).

I invented an elaborate mythology about the roof people. They were lost souls, I said, caught in a kind of purgatory. They lived in attics and on roofs. They were jealous of the living, and if they could find ways to trick us, to hurt us, they would. At night I would crawl out onto the roof and scratch at her window and then scramble back to my room so that I was innocently sitting at my desk by the time she arrived there in an angry panic. I take it as a point of pride that she slept with the lights on until she turned twenty-seven.

Life became a campfire story. I lost myself to books and movies, and even when I climbed out of them, their shadows stole across my life. Indeed, I pursued archaeology as a possible career purely because I fell in love with the Indiana Jones movies. I owned a fedora and a leather jacket and a satchel in which I kept bones and arrowheads and precious stones. I even bought a bullwhip and would practice snapping Coke cans off fenceposts. Then I spent a summer scouting rock-art sites for the Oregon Museum of Science and Industry—and another summer excavating a Paiute village with the

University of Oregon. But there were no rolling boulders, no booby traps or car chases, no Nazis to do battle with, no lost Ark of the Covenant waiting for me. There were certainly no beautiful women. There *were* snakes; I killed many of them with spears and ate their rubber-bandy meat and kept their rattles for charms. But the glare of the sun on my back as I hunched over a patch of sand and scraped through inch after inch of it only to discover a bone chip took its toll. The dream dissolved.

I went through a mild crisis, uncertain what to do with my life, and during this time I retreated to the woods. This was the summer of 1998, when all of my college buddies went off to New York internships, and I worked at Many Glacier Hotel in Glacier National Park. I was the gardener, a curious thing to be at a national park, and aside from deadheading geraniums and mowing the lawn, there wasn't a lot to do, so I spent most of my time on the clock sneaking into the women's dormitory and reading books and dreaming up stories in my toolshed. I had a leather-bound journal that I filled with my barbed-wire handwriting.

Most of these stories concerned bears. I saw them everywhere. When I mowed the lawn, I would count ten, twenty, thirty on the hillsides surrounding me, browsing for huckleberries. When I walked back from the employee bar at night, I would go stock-still and wait for the dark shape—the size of a VW bus—to trundle its way past me. When I camped in the backcountry, I would grip my knife and feel terror at the huffing noises outside my tent. We clapped and sang songs when we hiked. We carried pepper spray, which most people called seasoning, whenever we left blacktop. At the start of the summer, when I first stepped off the train, lugging my duffel, a ranger greeted me with the news that one of my colleagues had died. A mother and her cubs had mauled him, eaten him, leaving behind only his spine and his boots (with the feet still in them). These same bears would later stalk my roommate for ten miles, charging him and then turning away at the last second. They were hunted down, the mother killed and the cubs relocated. Bears haunted me. I dreamed of them—fighting them, escaping them, succumbing to them, becoming them—with the same sort of imaginative energy I had once applied to archaeology, and I drew from this dark well of experience when writing both my first novel, *The Wilding,* and my third, *The Dead Lands.*

But at this time, I was just playing around, dreaming with my eyes open—about bears and about a woman, a waitress who worked at the same lodge. She was five years older than me, a blue-eyed farm girl from Wisconsin. Every day, I wrote her a poem or a letter and snuck it into her employee mailbox. Sometimes I would spend the majority of my shift thinking about what I would write for her, pushing words around in my head. One day, when we were watching the sun set over the Rockies, she said, "You should become a writer," and I said, "Okay."

It was as though she had given me permission, clarified an impulse I hadn't been able to acknowledge or believe in, and I fell in love with her at the same time that I fell in love with the idea of devoting myself to the page. More than a decade later, you could say it's all been an attempt to impress a pretty girl, then my girlfriend, now my wife.

That was why I signed up for that first creative writing workshop, and soon enough I understood what my dead-faced professor meant when he said, "No genre."

Through his workshop—and the many workshops I took in the semesters to follow—I fell in love with writers I hadn't known existed, the writers who now fill my own syllabi. Flannery O'Connor, Sherman Alexie, Tim O'Brien, Raymond Carver, Alice Munro, James Baldwin. Take a look at the standard table of contents in any short-story anthology—I hadn't heard of any of them and I sought to remedy my ignorance. Every semester, on the first day, I heard the same warning, "No genre." Now I knew what the professors meant, and

I no longer cared, because I was caught in the tidal swirl of literary short fiction and devoted myself to reading and writing it exclusively.

Sentences were now more than vehicles for information; I pleasured in the arrangement of their words and read them aloud as if they were songs. Structures did not march forward with a chronological doggedness; they were cyclical or modular or framed or even arranged backward. Characters didn't act purely in the service of plot; they flirted their way into digressions, lingered in conversations and on windowsills, and in doing so became more than puppets, but as alive as anyone I knew.

I used to take pride in how quickly I could read. Because I was committed to story, to discovering what happened next, I turned the pages so swiftly they made a breeze on my face. In college, for the first time, I deliberately slowed down. Because despite all the books I had gobbled up, I didn't understand the careful carpentry of storytelling. Reading became less of an emotional experience and more of a mechanical inquiry. I kept a pen in hand, scribbling so many notes that the pages of my books appeared spiderwebbed.

I finally understood my high school English teacher, Mrs. O'Shea. She did her best to teach me, and I did my best to resist her. I remember, when we were reading *The Awakening,* by Kate Chopin, we got into a prolonged argument about symbolism. "The seagull doesn't mean anything," I said. "It's *just* a seagull. It's there for beach ambience."

I came across an essay a few years ago called "How We Listen to Music" by the composer Aaron Copland. He identifies three planes of listening. The first, the *sensuous plane,* is the simplest. You listen "for the sheer pleasure of the musical sound itself." I think it's safe to say that this is the way most people dial in to the radio—when blasting down the freeway or washing dishes in their kitchen—for background noise, something to tap their feet to, a way to manipulate their mood, to escape. I think it is also safe to say that this is the way most people read. Stories and music have that same potent, primitive force. We bend an ear toward them as distractions from the everyday.

The second plane he calls the *expressive*. The listener leans forward instead of leaning back. They discern the expressive power of the notes and lyrics. Are there satanic messages and *Lord of the Rings* references nested in "Stairway to Heaven"? What does Bob Dylan mean when he sings, "I saw a white ladder all covered with water"? What is the piece trying to say? What is the piece *about*?

The third plane most listeners are not conscious of, what Copland identifies as the *sheerly musical*. The way music "does exist in terms of the notes themselves and of their manipulation." The rhythm, the melody, the harmonies, the tone colors—the principles of musical form and orchestration—what you can identify only through training and deep concentration.

Not all at once, but slowly, slowly, like a snake shedding its skin, I broke through each of these planes as a writer by first becoming a strenuous reader, able to engage with a text with critical literacy. Whereas before I had been committed purely to the sensuous, now I could recognize the larger orchestration of notes, the mechanics of the component parts. I understood that the seagull was in fact much more than a seagull—so that I am now able to bow my head and say, "Mrs. O'Shea, I'm sorry."

Years passed. I sold many of my dragon and ghost and robot books back to Powell's and used the in-store credit to fill the empty space on my shelves with Andrea Barrett and Joan Didion and Rick Bass and Harry Crews. I entered graduate school. I woke up every morning before dawn to write. I fell asleep every evening with a book on my chest and ink spots on my sheets. I began to publish regularly in small literary journals.

And then one day I realized I was bored.

In 2003, when I was muscling my way through grad school, Michael Chabon edited a book called *McSweeney's Mammoth Treasury of*

Thrilling Tales. All of the stories—written by Aimee Bender, Dan Chaon, Kelly Link, Stephen King, Elmore Leonard, and many others, a fine mix of so-called "literary" and so-called "genre" writers—leaned into daring plots and narrative action, battling the current trend toward stories that are "plotless and sparkling with epiphanic dew," as Chabon writes in his introduction.

Sherman Alexie writes about zombies. Jim Shepard writes about a giant shark. Kelly Link writes about witches, Rick Moody about drugs that send you back in time to relive memories, Nick Hornby about a magic VCR that fast-forwards you into an apocalyptic future. I was spellbound. Not because the stories are earthshakingly good (though some are), but because Chabon ganged together all of these heavyweights and asked them to write the kind of stories that had made them want to become writers in the first place.

When I imagined my own name in the table of contents, when I wondered what kind of story I would have written for Chabon, I felt a surprised recognition, as if I had flipped open an old photo album and spotted an image of me I had forgotten existed. *This* was what I wanted to do, *this* was the kind of writer I hoped to be, but somewhere along the way I had lost the path. My classes, while very valuable to me, taught me to fetishize sentences and theme and character. Nobody ever used the word *plot,* as if it were something rank or forbidden. And nobody in my workshop ever snuck a zombie or a zeppelin or a giant shark into their stories, for fear of them being labeled *genre,* the ultimate insult in so many creative writing programs.

I then read Chabon's epic Pulitzer Prize–winning novel, *The Amazing Adventures of Kavalier and Clay*—a wonder of escapism that holds nothing back, its language as magically exuberant as the plot, which revolves around comic books, Nazis, golems, Antarctic battles—and I understood him as a writer who transcended boundaries.

These days, literary fiction is largely owned by the academy, and academics are obsessed with taxonomy. Go to the Association of

Writers and Writing Programs (AWP) conference sometime if you want proof of this. Most of the panels consist of people trying to figure out what to call something or someone—postmodernism, new masculinity, magical realism, post-industrialism; Midwest writer, mother writer, Asian writer, Caribbean writer, war writer—and what that label might require. I know labels make people feel better in a neat-freaky sort of way. Like balling their socks and organizing them in a drawer according to color. And I know it's a talking point, a frame for discussion. But really, you nerdy fussbudget, when you start to worry about whether someone is literary or genre, or literary crossover (whatever that means), you are devoting valuable brain energy to something that ultimately doesn't matter. These are phantom barricades that serve only to restrict.

What is Michael Chabon? What is Margaret Atwood? Or Kate Atkinson? Or Cormac McCarthy? Or Octavia Butler? Or Peter Straub, Larry McMurtry, Ursula K. Le Guin, Tom Franklin, Susannah Clarke? Or, or, or? You could argue these writers into several different corners of the bookstore, and the same can be said if you look even further back—before the rise of the creative writing program—at the canonized likes of Shirley Jackson or Raymond Chandler or Ray Bradbury or Nathaniel Hawthorne or Henry James. If I am going to align myself with anyone, it's them. And anyone else who makes an effort to be both a writer *and* a storyteller, someone who puts their muscle into artful technique and compulsive readability.

Realism is the trend. That's what Chabon helped me realize. That's what the academy—the institutionalization of creative writing—has forgotten. Look back on the long, hoof-marked trail of literature. The beastly majority of stories contain elements of the fantastic. It's only very recently that realism has become the dominant mode. And that's changing, thanks to people like Chabon, who has been a cheerleader for plotted fiction, for more hybridized vigor and playfulness, and thanks to the rise of writers like George Saunders and Karen Russell and Kevin Brockmeier and Kate Bernheimer, who are neither fish nor fowl, both literary and genre. Call it the Avengerization of literature.

In fifth grade, for Christmas, I gave my teacher a mason jar full of neon-green ectoplasm dotted with plastic spiders. Her desk was festooned with glittery gift bags, ribboned boxes, a fruit basket padded with cotton balls meant to look like snow. I did not wrap the mason jar, so Mrs. Hen knew what she was getting, but still she asked me, "What is it?"

"It's a jar full of ectoplasm," I said proudly. "With spiders." At home, on my bedside table, I kept my own jar, and every night I would hold the goo up to my lamp and make it glow, rotating it in my hands, studying the dark matter speckling it. I considered it pretty much the coolest thing ever, right up there with my Tales from the Crypt comics collection and the poster on my door of an alien tearing through a door.

Mrs. Hen picked up the jar, tipped it at an angle that matched her cocked head, and together we shared a quiet moment as the ectoplasm oozed and found a new shape. A bubble burped from its bottom. "It's so . . . ," Mrs. Hen said, and that's all she said, because the bell rang and she stood from her desk while I scurried to mine.

If the bell had not rung, if that moment in time had extended itself another few seconds, what might Mrs. Hen have said? "It's so . . . extraordinary"? Beautiful? Arousing?

I like to think so. I like to think she still has the jar on display, maybe in some prized location, her fireplace mantle, the centerpiece of her dining room table. But I know better. I know, in all likelihood, she would have said "different."

The jar was *different.* I was *different.* This is a word I hear often in the Midwest—in response to a film, a book, a spicy dish—a meek way of saying, "Not good. Weird. Abnormal."

Sometimes people ask about my parents. As if I grew up in a cobwebby Victorian with bats in the attic and chain saws in the basement.

As if I were Eddie Munster or Pugsley Addams. But this is not the case.

If I am a product of anyone, it is writers like Ray Bradbury, Octavia Butler, Stephen King, Richard Matheson. Whether parents or gods, they are legion, storytellers with marred minds that begat altered realities more compelling and somehow truer than life. They were *different,* and I read them in the poorly lit corners of libraries and I read them in bed when storms boomed outside, sometimes spending more of my time daydreaming in a book than engaging with the world. Their pages were like holographic chambers full of dragons, ghosts, aliens that became my reality, rewiring my brain to celebrate and anticipate the fantastic.

When hiking in the woods, I would strike a tree with a stick three times and tell my sister that was how you called Bigfoot. When playing on the beach, I imagined the long, tuberous seaweed as the tentacles of a kraken. When eating at a restaurant, the waiters and the chef became cannibals who kept a kitchen storage locker full of bodies from which they hacked steaks and chops. I am *different,* and it is this difference that compels me to propose an aesthetic barometer. Let's call it the Exploding Helicopter Clause.

If a story does not contain an exploding helicopter, an editor will not publish it, no matter how pretty its sentences and orgasmic its epiphany might be. The exploding helicopter is an inclusive term that may refer but is not limited to giant sharks, robots with laser eyes, pirates, poltergeists, were-kittens, demons, slow zombies, fast zombies, talking unicorns, probe-wielding martians, sexy vampires, barbarians in hairy underwear, and all forms of apocalyptic and postapocalyptic mayhem.

I'm joking, but I'm not. I'm embracing what so many journals and workshops seem allergic to. Go ahead. Complain about genre. You're allowed. The worst of it features formulaic plots, pedestrian language, paper-thin characters, gender and ethnic stereotypes, and a general lack of diversity. I, too, cringe and stifle a laugh when I read lines like this: "Renowned curator Jacques Saunière staggered through the vaulted archway of the museum's Grand Gallery."

But while we're at it, let's complain about literary fiction. The *worst* of it features a pile of pretty sentences that add up to nothing happening. Maybe a marital spat is followed by someone drinking tea and remembering some distant precious moment and then gazing out the window at a roiling bank of clouds that gives them a visual counterpoint to their heart-trembling, loin-shivering epiphany.

It's easy to grouse and make fun. Flip the equation and study what works best instead. Literary fiction highlights exquisite sentences, glowing metaphors, subterranean themes, fully realized characters. And genre fiction excels at raising *the* most important question: *What happens next? What happens next?* is why most people read. It's what makes us fall in love with books and makes some of us hope to write one of our own someday, though we may have forgotten that if we've fallen under the indulgent spell of our pretty sentences.

Toss out the worst elements of genre and literary fiction—and merge the best. We might then create a new taxonomy, so that when you walk into a bookstore, the stock is divided into "Stories that suck" and "Stories that will make your mind and heart explode with their goodness."

Many years ago, I was lucky enough to study under Barry Hannah, whose voice in person and on the page was equivalent to a jazz saxophone on an ear-burning riff. On the final day of workshop, I asked him if he had any parting wisdom, and he licked his lips and narrowed his eyes and gave me the best advice of my life: "Thrill me."

Urgency

I had a buddy in high school named Darren, and the first time we met, he asked me, "How do you make a tissue dance?" I didn't know. Neither did he. The question had haunted him since fifth grade. That was when he visited Six Flags, and while waiting in line for a roller coaster, a hand fell on his shoulder. It belonged to a man with slicked-back hair and aviator shades that reflected Darren's own startled face. "Hey, kid," the man said. "How do you make a tissue dance?"

"I don't know," Darren said. "How?" At that moment the line pushed forward and the man fell away and Darren shrugged him off as a weirdo. Twenty minutes later, when Darren finally climbed into the coaster and locked the safety bar into place, he heard a voice calling out, "Hey, kid!" There was the man, leaning against the metal railing, grinning at Darren with too many white teeth. "How do you make a tissue dance?"

The coaster lurched forward, chugging its way up, up, up toward that first stomach-swooning drop—but Darren found himself distracted, barely able to enjoy the ride, even as he roared along, as he looped and swooped and felt like his guts might unspool through his throat, because down below, among the many bodies, he could make out the man—watching him—mouthing the words "How do you make a tissue dance?"

When the coaster rattled to a stop, Darren climbed out and

chased through the crowds, hunting for the man, but he was gone, never to be seen again. How *do* you make a tissue dance? Because the answer escaped him, it seemed vitally important, as if he might discover in a dancing tissue the meaning of life, the origins of the universe. Note that this happened before Google, and for the next several years he would ask everyone he met, including me, "How do you make a tissue dance?"

I could tell you the answer. But I won't. Not yet.

You would regret inviting me on vacation. I am that person, the one everyone hates, who carves out every minute of every day. We will rise at dawn to mainline espresso and bike a five-mile canyon so that by ten we can race through the museum and then get lunch at that taco stand on the other side of town before pounding out an ocean-side hike before touring the haunted lighthouse before diving into a shipwreck before snarfing sushi before the bluegrass concert before the whiskey bar before the amazing sex we will enjoy at the stroke of midnight.

Hell, to me, is a cruise ship. Hell is lying on a beach with no plan outside of soaking up a few rays, sucking down a few piña coladas. Hell is relaxing. I cannot sit still. I am never not doing something. Even when watching a movie, I answer emails and do crunches and jot down notes on a yellow legal tablet.

Needless to say, this does not serve me well in personal relationships. Nobody likes a guy who can't chill out, take it easy. I never stop working. I am always . . . desiring. But my busyness finds a healthy outlet in my fiction—no matter which direction my prose is headed, the engine rarely idles.

I. Establish a Clear Narrative Goal

You already know this. Kill the whale. Stop the serial killer. Save the world from the doomsday asteroid. Travel to Mordor, to Mount Doom to hurl the ring of power into the fiery chasm from whence it came.

These are higher-order goals, which give a narrative its larger propulsive arc. Writers do a decent job of figuring this out. Their characters throw their duffel bags into the back of a truck and growl off on a road trip to Boise, Idaho. Their characters, doomed by lust, pursue lovers outside their marriage. Their characters clean and oil their rifles as they plan the murder of someone next in line for promotion.

But they often forget that alongside this narrative goal, you must create a sense of human urgency.

II. Human Urgency

Imagine the emotional arc of your character laid upon the narrative arc of the story. To create suspense, you must have both: what is outside of the character (whatever is intruding on her life) and inside of the character (whatever she desires that is just out of her reach). When these two things come together, you build the potential for something to happen.

The actor says to the director, "What's my motivation?" Your characters ask the same of you. Chief Brody in Peter Benchley's *Jaws* is motivated to kill the shark for professional reasons (that star on his chest and the pistol at his belt obligate him to protect Amity Island and its citizens) and for personal reasons (he is a neglectful husband whose wife is having an affair and the pursuit of the shark serves as an outlet for him to counter his sense of powerlessness and emasculation).

Ree Dolly in Daniel Woodrell's *Winter's Bone* is motivated to find her father for three reasons: financial (he has put up their house and land for bail), familial (she has been left to care for her brain-dead mother and two younger brothers), and ideological (she needs to step up in a way her father never has, test her mettle against lawmen and outlaws alike, and in doing so overcome the staunchly patriarchal culture of the Ozarks).

These are the stakes of the situation. Whether financial, professional, emotional, physical, or spiritual, they give your character a reason to go on their journey—and they give us a reason to follow. No stakes means no urgency means a stillborn story.

III. Create Obstacles that Ramp Up the Tension

Consider *The Lovely Bones,* by Alice Sebold, a novel about the murder of a teenage girl named Susie Salmon who observes her family from the afterlife as they come to terms with her death. Her sister, Lindsey Salmon, correctly believes that their creepy neighbor—a dollhouse-maker named George Harvey—is the murderer. She makes it her mission to prove this.

One day, on a run through the neighborhood with her cross-country team, she notices Harvey's car pulling away. This is her chance to upend his house in a search for clues. She darts into his side yard (our first point of tension) as she worries that her teammates will notice she is no longer running alongside them. She kicks in the basement window (the second point of tension), the chiming burst of glass loud enough to alert the neighbors. When she worms through the narrow opening, we fear the glass will cut her (our third point of tension—I'll stop counting now; you get the idea). The basement is shadow-soaked, many of the lightbulbs dead. She finds nothing of interest, so she tromps upstairs and yanks open drawers and cupboards, all the while worrying over when Harvey might return. A few minutes later, now in his bedroom on the second story, she is ready to give up, when a floorboard creaks beneath her foot.

She pries it up—and discovers, in the recess beneath, a notebook. Its pages are full of sketches and tidy handwriting that detail *exactly* how Harvey captured, raped, and murdered Susie Salmon. She tucks the floorboard back into place and readies herself to leave. Mission accomplished.

But no. Just then an engine is heard outside. A car pulls into the driveway: Harvey. Lindsey is trapped upstairs as Harvey enters the house, sets down his groceries, and notices an open cabinet door. He knows immediately someone has been in the house—and when

Lindsey steps on the loose floorboard in his bedroom and it emits a groan, he pounds upstairs to seize her.

After finding the notebook, after facing so many obstacles, she is permitted only a second's relief. Her goal now shifts from "get the evidence" to "get out alive," a nice reversal. She yanks open the window. Not only does she have to lean across a desk to reach it, but she discovers it's locked. She manages to sneak out before Harvey can grab her—but of course she slips on the shingles and rolls off the roof. The impact of her fall knocks the breath from her and she lies paralyzed in the grass. Harvey explodes out the front door, his arms outstretched, clawing for her, just as she manages to stumble up and sprint away. In this one set-piece moment, I lost track of the number of obstacles, they mounted so swiftly.

This is where you always want to put your characters: in the tight spot from which escape seems nearly impossible. And this scene—in the murderer's home—is one of hundreds in the novel when characters chase answers.

IV. Create Lower-Order Goals

Lower-order goals drive your scenes. Stacie needs to get to the store to buy beer for the graduation party. Johnny needs to sneak out of his parents' house one night to meet up with a girl. Sam needs to hammer plywood over the windows before the hurricane arrives. Think of these as micro finish lines, something for readers to constantly race toward. Any marathon runner knows that though their goal is to cross the finish line, they keep their desire piqued by racing for that concrete bench just up ahead, a crooked street sign at the end of the street, a yellow dog tied to a parking meter on the corner of the next street, the thousand tiny accomplishments that add up to a victory.

Lower-order goals are especially important to consider when writing dialogue. Unlike other forms of characterization, such as appearance ("He wore the kind of crushed-velvet leisure suit favored by Florida retirees") or gesture ("She marched into the room and stomped her foot to seize our attention") or decision ("The boy did not call out for his mother but watched, almost curiously, as his sister choked on the damp hunk of broccoli"), dialogue generally distinguishes itself as pure, unfiltered, straight from the source, without a narrator to manipulate it. Perhaps this is why so many writers feel they can wallow in dialogue, especially in novels. They set their characters down on a park bench—or at a dimly lit bar, or in a rusted-out Datsun—and away they go, yakety-yak yakking for pages on end. Not only is this chattiness excessive, often redundant (we *understand* that the father is a prick and the son a pushover after four lines), and expository (we *don't want* characters to go on and on explaining their troubled history or how the museum painting contains a stupid code), but also it destroys momentum.

If you must have a protracted verbal exchange, then, damn it, give your characters something to do. By that I do *not* mean give them a cigarette or a beer. I mean make them grill a steak or attend a carnival or splat together a papier-mâché volcano or inch their car through a long stretch of construction. Bob needs to get to the store to buy the Christmas ham. Bertha needs to escape the cobwebbed dungeon. When you want to include a scene of long-lasting dialogue (in which the husband will reveal he had sex with his masseuse or a grandfather will explain how he lost his foot when he stepped on a land mine in Korea), try to superimpose it on something else, something with a finish line—a lower-order goal.

The outcome of the conversation (Character A wants to reveal his feelings to Character B, for example) is almost never enough. To make the audience want to push forward, to wonder what happens next, there needs to be something else at work. The lower-order goal will serve that function, providing a healthy dose of momentum.

Consider the work of Thomas Harris, an author of smart, psychologically rich thrillers, including *The Silence of the Lambs*. He can certainly teach the literary writer a thing or two about pacing. In his novel *Red Dragon,* he introduces the character Francis Dolarhyde. After Francis brings home his (kind of) girlfriend, Reba McClane, the two have an intimate conversation in his living room. While sucking down martinis, they talk about the history of his house (a former nursing home), the insecurity he feels about his speech and appearance (he was born with a cleft palate), and the romantic spark between them. (Is he interested? She certainly is.) On its own, this scene would be only vaguely compelling, but as Harris has written it, the reader can barely breathe. Reba is blind, and while she and Francis talk, he readies and then silently plays a home video of a family he murdered. The conversation takes on a whole new meaning as we wonder whether Reba will make Francis walk the straight and narrow or if he will chew off her face.

Beyond pacing, there is also the issue of tone. Flip through a novel. Take a visual inventory of the way it's arranged. Dialogue is peppered throughout, but most of the paragraphs are meaty blocks of action and summary that house the voice of the book, a voice whose tone and diction are typically established by the end of the first paragraph and maintained thereafter. When writers settle into the park bench scene—or the bar stool scene or the kitchen table scene—the characters' dialogue takes over, resulting in a narrative coup. On a basic level, we feel unmoored from the book and its tonal contract. But when you triangulate prolonged dialogue—when you interrupt it, center it around some goal-driven action—you are constantly grounding your audience, reminding them of the book's timbre, maintaining your tonal contract.

Graham Greene is a master of this. Look at *The Power and the Glory.* Read any portion of that remarkable book, really, but for the sake of example, the second part of the first chapter, in which the whiskey priest is reunited with his former lover and abandoned child and lingers in the village to give communion even as the police pursue him. Back and forth we go between the awkward snippets of dialogue ("You didn't recognize me?" "You've changed.") and the sections of narrative that stress the emotional weight of his visit (the sight of his daughter clogs his mind with guilt) and the physical peril of it (he hears a soldier's horse whinny, moving through the mist toward him).

Tone refers not only to voice but to music, the foot-tapping rhythm of the words. Dialogue is typically staccato, while narrative is typically legato. To linger too long in the choppiness of dialogue disrupts the smoothly connected paragraphs of the narrative. An uninterrupted string of dialogue between two characters can be as exhausting as a single key struck repeatedly on the piano. But Samantha's impassioned plea for forgiveness interrupted by Joe's slow, methodical arrangement of a house of cards has enough rhythmic interruptions to keep us tonally engaged, like any carefully constructed orchestration.

The lower-order goal will also—if you're good—serve as a metaphoric backdrop and enhance characterization. Let's say Brian is still pissed at Jimmy for marrying his high school sweetheart, Lauren. Perhaps this point of tension, secreted away for so many years, comes to a head on a hunting trip. They both have knives—they're gutting and skinning a buck, sectioning the meat—when Jimmy starts to bother Brian about his dating habits. "You never make an effort," he says. "What about that bartender at the Pine Tavern? She's got eyes for you." The way Brian saws hurriedly through a joint—or lets his knife slip to puncture the gut sack and spoil the meat—is as full of meaning as anything he might say aloud.

This is a form of misdirection. Your characters are avoiding (and revealing through avoidance) their true feelings. Instead of discussing their steadily disintegrating marriage, a wife and husband argue about fertilizer while weeding in the garden. Instead of telling a teacher how he hates her, a first grader draws a pool of blood in red crayon and tells her it's a sun. Kent Haruf offers up a more charming example of this in *Plainsong,* when the old McPheron brothers go shopping for a crib and baby supplies. These characters spend most of their days outside, spreading manure in the fields and bucking hay bales into the back of pickup trucks, and seem ridiculously out of place in a department store. They're there only for Victoria Roubideaux, a pregnant teenager abandoned by her mother and by the father of her baby. The brothers have taken her into their home—and now into town—because they love her as a daughter. Not that they would ever say such a thing. But the way they banter gruffly with the retail clerk ("Why ever would you want hooded casters?" "For decoration." "Ma'am?" "It looks better." "I expect that's important, how the wheels look.") and then seek out the most stylish, expensive crib ("You have this in stock, I guess.") comes to represent their love. The conversation—triangulated around a shopping expedition—is as close as they'll ever come to a heart-to-heart talk with Victoria.

Perhaps the most *exciting* use of triangulation comes from the HBO series *Game of Thrones*. The novels in the Fire and Ice saga by George R. R. Martin are packed with characters, crammed with histories, each volume as big as a brick. Showrunner David Benioff has to crush a lot of intel into his hour-long episodes without the benefit of interiority or an omniscient narrator to fill us in on trade routes, family grudges, political scandals, the customs of different regions. So the task goes to the characters. They tell each other (and the eavesdropping audience) what needs to be known. But expository dialogue is, of course, clunky and boring. Benioff distracts us from this by using sex as a triangulating device. Two bodies will be entangled in a bath or pressed up against a wall or perched on the edge of a bed strewn with furs—and as they're manipulating their hands or readjusting their hips, they'll talk (about politics and war, usually), punctuating their sentences with the occasional moan or gasp. Call it sexpository dialogue. Or sexposition. The power struggle between the two lovers usually reflects the subject matter: Littlefinger rants about power while luxuriously watching two prostitutes audition for his brothel; Margaery Tyrell offers herself to her husband,

Renly Baratheon, and when she cannot arouse him so that they might conceive an heir, she is not offended but clear-eyed and strategic, talking about their future—the future of the realm, their future as king and queen—and she then invites Ser Loras, the Knight of Flowers, into their tent to help excite her husband.

No matter how beautiful or ugly your characters are, no matter how charming or obnoxious, quiet or noisy, no matter what their purpose in a given scene, the reasoning behind triangulating dialogue is simple: always have more than one thing going on in your fiction. And if the triangle is the strongest, most basic self-reinforcing structure, then consider this a lesson in the geometry of dialogue.

V. Ticking Clock

As your character negotiates these obstacles and crosses these micro finish lines, I strongly advise that you create a ticking clock. The boys must lose their virginity before graduation. The athlete must get in shape before the big fight. The miners must be rescued before they run out of air. The pilot must make it across the sea before the tank runs out of fuel. The quarantine must occur before the virus spreads out of the town. Cinderella must woo her prince by midnight.

I work well under deadline. There is something about the watch on my wrist, the calendar on the wall, that energizes me. Because I have *only so much time*. This kind of urgency carries over to fiction, where a ticking clock—a sense of time running out—can make the pages seem to snap by with the speed of a second hand.

The most exaggerated version of this might come from Poe's "The Pit and the Pendulum." As the paragraphs progress, the blade flashes lower and lower, making the reader suck in their stomach for fear of a slash.

A close cousin to this might be the black monolith that appears in the sky—in the opening section of Kevin Brockmeier's short story "The Ceiling"—slowly descending until it blots away the sun and reaches from horizon to horizon and threatens to crush the characters. Or the pieces of paper, one of them stained black with a death sentence, in Shirley Jackson's story "The Lottery." Or the bush plane, in Pam Houston's novel *Contents May Have Shifted,* which coughs and empties its fuel tank and must find a lake to land on in the thick-forested Alaskan wilderness. In David Benioff's novel *The 25th Hour,* the protagonist experiences one final day of freedom before serving a seven-year prison sentence. And in the film *The Descendants,* George Clooney's comatose wife will die two weeks after he pulls the plug on her. This is the reason the long-running TV show *24* had such breathless pacing, its clock steadily ticking its way down to zero.

In all these examples, there is a doomsday clock that indicates danger and the possibility of avoidance. But the device need not be so sinister. There are more understated ways to suggest time's passage.

Consider the opening of Hemingway's *The Old Man and the Sea:* "He was an old man who fished alone in a skiff in the Gulf Stream and he had gone eighty-four days now without taking a fish." We know, after such a long wait, it is only a matter of time. And when the bite finally does come, and the tug-of-war rages, we know it is only a matter of time before the man or the fish gives up.

Or consider "A Temporary Matter" by Jhumpa Lahiri, which begins with the line "The notice informed them that it was a temporary matter: for five days their electricity would be cut off for one hour, beginning at eight P.M." The husband and wife, their child lost, their marriage in ruins, must dine together by candlelight and with only their conversation to keep them company, an intimacy they had forgotten. And by the end of those five days, we come to understand, their relationship will either mend itself or terminate.

Christopher Coake's short story "All through the House," Martin Amis's novel *Time's Arrow,* and Christopher Nolan's film *Memento* reinvent the doomsday timer device by composing their narratives in reverse, all of them ticking their way down to zero, where something terrible usually awaits.

There is an expiration date, of course. What if Cinderella had until midnight . . . seven days from now to woo her prince? What if Jesus was in the wilderness for four thousand days instead of forty? What if the teenagers in *Superbad* had to lose their virginity before they graduated from PhD programs in Germanic literature instead of during their remaining days of high school?

I used this strategy of harried anticipation throughout my new novel, *Red Moon*, but nowhere more explicitly than in the opening chapter. A man—dressed in a sharply creased suit and shoes polished black as opals—enters an airport. His briefcase is empty. His neck razor-burned. He breathes fiercely through his nose and paces constantly and sweats so heavily that when he dabs at his forehead with his boarding pass, the ink bleeds. There is enough prognostication—with his reflection like a ghost in the rain-flecked window and the overhead compartments gaping like unhinged jaws—that the reader *knows* something terrible is coming. And it comes, fifteen agonizing pages later, a long fuse sizzling its way toward a brick of dynamite.

VI. Delay Gratification and Withhold Information

Remember my buddy Darren? The one who wanted to know—so desperately—how to make a tissue dance? Senior year of high school, I worked at an athletic club, a high-end facility where everyone drove BMWs, wore boat shoes, and was named Tad. I mowed the lawn, maintained the weight and cardio equipment, and occasionally helped out in the locker room. That's where I was—spraying mirrors, refilling soap dispensers, picking up towels—when I heard a voice say, "Hey, Tad—here's a good one for you. How do you make a tissue dance?"

I dropped my armload of towels and listened in stunned silence. The answer—at last!—revealed. Because I am a true son of a bitch, afterward I told Darren I knew the punch line but refused to share it. I'll admit our friendship suffered. I wanted to torture him, sure, but I also wanted to prolong the reveal.

We know this from the bedroom. If a seduction goes on for weeks, months—if clothes peel off slowly—if nails and lips tease before taking hold—if patience gradually gives way to forcefulness— the more explosive the results, the more gratitude we feel.

In this same fashion the detective novel follows a trail of clues before revealing whodunit. And in this same fashion Grover, in *The Monster at the End of This Book,* ties ropes across pages, builds brick walls, continually warning the reader about the monster at the end of the book, heightening our fear and spiking our relief when we flip to the final page and discover the monster is none other than furry, lovable Grover.

You might apply this same strategy to your most interesting characters by building up their offstage mythology. Many westerns begin with some equivalent of the following: the hero rides into town, stables his horse, moseys into the saloon, orders a whiskey, and plops down for a card game. After a few hands, someone will mention Rattlesnake Pete, and our hero will say, "Who?" and everyone at the table will gulp and look around nervously before a one-eyed, unshaven scoundrel with no teeth will say in a rusted-out voice, "Mean to tell me you never heard of Rattlesnake Pete? He eats diamondbacks for breakfast and pisses venom and killed six men with one bullet!" No doubt we'll hear about old Rattlesnake Pete three or four more times before his spur-jangling boots finally stomp into view and the camera tracks up his body—past his snakeskin holsters, his rattle-festooned vest, to his scarred face, at which point he'll fire an oyster of tobacco from his mouth and we'll flinch because we've been trained to fear him.

J. K. Rowling pulls the same move in *Harry Potter and the Sorcerer's Stone.* First Hagrid on the island and then the wand-maker in Diagon Alley and then Ron Weasley on the train and then the students and professors at Hogwarts tell Harry about You-Know-Who, a.k.a. He-Who-Must-Not-Be-Named (a villain whose offstage my-thology is so profound even his name remains in the shadows). The constant references are akin to a grumbling thunder that anticipates the storm to come in the final act, when Professor Quirrell's turban unravels to reveal Voldemort's snakelike visage.

Lauren Groff treats Spanish influenza similarly in her short story "L. DeBard and Aliette." On the first page, she feeds us a line: "It is March 1918, and hundreds of dead jellyfish litter the beach. The morning newspapers include a story, buried under the accounts of battles at the Western Front, about a mysterious illness striking down hale soldiers in Kansas." Not only is the report buried in the newspaper; it's buried in the opening scene, so that at first glance it seems merely to contextualize rather than foreshadow. But four pages later, Groff brings it up again. "While L. and Aliette wait to begin their first lesson the next day, the mysterious illness is creep-ing from the sleepy Spanish tourist town of San Sebastián. It will make its way into the farthest corners of the realm, until even King Alfonso XIII will lie suffering in his royal bed. French, English, and American troops scattered in France are just now becoming deathly ill, and the disease will skulk with them to England. Even King George V will be afflicted."

Now we're worried. The second, lingering mention of the dis-ease makes it clear that it will play some sinister role in the narra-tive. It is another six pages before we hear about it again: "In late April, the newspapers are full of news of a strange illness. The jour-nalists try to blunt their alarm by exoticizing it, naming it Spanish influenza, *La Grippe*. In Switzerland, it is called *La Coquette,* as if it were a courtesan. In Ceylon it's the Bombay Fever, and in Britain the Flanders Grippe. The Germans, whom the Allies blame for this disease, call it *Blitzkatarrh*. The disease is as stealthy as that name sounds.

"Americans do not pay attention. They watch Charlie Chaplin and laugh until they cry. They read the sports pages and make bets on when the war will be over. And if a few healthy soldiers suddenly fall ill and die, the Americans blame it on exposure to tear gas."

Of course it will finger its way into the United States, into New York, into the doomed love affair of our titular characters. The way Groff treats the flu reminds me of the way the TV networks treat superstorms. How often do we hear about a hurricane as it swirls across the Atlantic, as it gains power, as newscasters weigh hypotheticals as to where it might come ashore and the lives and property it will threaten?

One day, after graduation, toward the end of summer, Darren and I and a bunch of our miscreant pals hauled a speedboat out to Lake Billy Chinook for one last hurrah. In a few weeks, we would climb onto airplanes and fly off to different colleges, and this was our way of saying so long. We drank some beers and hit on some girls and tore through the reservoir on our skis. It was then—as Darren jumped the wake and kicked up a big rooster tail of water— that I decided to finally give him the answer to the question that had vexed him for so long. Over the motor I yelled, "How do you make a tissue dance?" I could tell by the widening of his eyes that he knew it was time. I would finally give him his answer. This was the moment he had been waiting for.

So . . .

How do you make a tissue dance?

You put a little boogie in it.

And with that, his eight-year mission had come to an end. Darren released the towrope and fell back into the water and let Lake Billy Chinook swallow him up with a look of utter disappointment on his face.

You're disappointed, too. That's because desire is the most thrilling and pleasurable and terrifying condition. Anticipation satisfies us in a way acquisition does not. The day after Thanksgiving, when we tromp into the Minnesota woods and saw down a Christmas tree, my kids are beside themselves, almost shivering with excitement, formulating their wish lists, daydreaming about Santa diving down the chimney with a bag full of gifts. Every morning of December, they sprint to the Advent calendar for their chocolate and count the days remaining. On Christmas Eve, they become almost feverish, their eyes darting between the tree and the fireplace. But when the twenty-fifth finally comes, after they pound down the stairs, after they wake me with their shrieks, after they make confetti of the wrapping paper, their demeanor suddenly shifts. A long quiet spell follows. They slump among the broken shells of boxes and gaze sadly at the empty space beneath the tree.

It's the way we're wired. We need to have something to look forward to. Prizes are shiniest before they're won, just as monsters are scariest before they're seen. That is why Melville kept his white whale hidden so long, a shadowy surge, a pale mass breaking the surface in the distance. Jules Verne treated his sea-shrouded squid in the same way. This is the power of temporary blindness.

Stephen King says that the most terrifying moment in any horror story comes when a character hears a noise—behind an attic or basement door, beyond a thicket, deep in a cave—and pursues it. We always want to yell out: "Don't go there!" It's that moment of suspense, the second before the bogeyman is revealed, that is the most arresting. After the door opens, after the flashlight shines on whatever creature lies in wait, the audience might laugh or scream but ultimately they feel relief. Because it's never as bad as what they imagined.

But there's a way to fight this sense of disappointment, the Christmas morning blues. Consider this common trait among Rattlesnake Pete and Voldemort and Spanish influenza. Their eventual appearance in the narrative does not eliminate tension but instead exacerbates it, encouraging more trouble, introducing greater mysteries.

That's how my favorite scene works in Cormac McCarthy's *The Road*. As soon as the father spots the house on the hill, we know something terrible waits inside. It takes a long time for him to approach the rotten building, to explore its many rooms, and finally to descend into the basement.

"He started down the rough wooden steps. He ducked his head and then flicked the lighter and swung the flame out over the darkness like an offering. Coldness and damp. An ungodly stench. He could see part of a stone wall. Clay floor. An old mattress darkly stained. He crouched and stepped down again and held out the light."

The whole time we're yelling: "Don't go in there!"

But he does. Of course he does:

Huddled against the back wall were naked people, male and female, all trying to hide, shielding their faces with their hands. On the mattress lay a man with his legs gone to the hip and the stumps of them blackened and burnt. The smell was hideous.

Jesus, he whispered.

Then one by one they turned and blinked in the pitiful light. Help us, they whispered. Please help us.

Yes, it's a long, slow, suspense-deepening, stakes-raising period of temporary blindness. He withholds information and the sentences progress like a spitting fuse that leads toward a detonation. But here's the thing that really makes it work. The first mystery (what's in the basement) opens the door to another mystery (who put the freaks there). These pale, chewed-up creatures emerge from the dark and rattle their chains and moan and reach for the father. We're afraid of them, but we're more afraid of what awaits the father upstairs— the people responsible for their imprisonment. Humans are harvesting each other in order to survive. If the father doesn't blaze out of this place, his son is going to end up seasoned and diced into a Salisbury steak.

There is a shelf life for every mystery. No one keeps a twelve-month Advent calendar (even twenty-five days can sometimes feel painfully long for most of us grinches). The shark eventually has to push out of the ocean and give us a chum-stained grin. The telltale heart can beat only so many times before we lose patience and say, "Come on, already—get over your conscience or give yourself up to the cops."

Gauge the importance of what you're hiding and relegate an appropriate number of pages before the reveal. Darren's quest to discover the answer to the question "How do you make a tissue dance?" lasted too long and inflated its importance, which made the disappointing punch line even more unsatisfactory. But in a way every answer is unsatisfactory unless it opens up into another question. Which means a good story is a turnstile of mysteries. Once one is solved, another ought to swing forcefully into the narrative.

Here's an example, lifted from a script I wrote for *Detective Comics.* An overseas flight won't respond to air traffic control as it approaches the Gotham International Airport. Mystery #1: what the hell is going on? Mechanical problem? Terrorist threat? What?

This question has a short shelf life. The plane can remain up in the air only so long. During the next few panicked pages, we realize it's too late for the F-14s to take to the sky, so the Port Authority and the TSA officers line up on the runway, ready for action, while all other flights are grounded and cleared from the tarmac. The plane finally appears, comes to a skidding halt, and crashes through an atrium window, maiming several passengers who are lounging on couches and ordering lattes at a coffee stand. The stakes keep ratcheting up. Meanwhile, Bruce Wayne is readying for takeoff in his private jet, so he leaps into action as Batman.

The cockpit windshield and the porthole windows of the mystery flight remain dark. No movement is observed within. Batman rips open the cabin door and discovers . . . everyone on board is dead! And old. Withered, gray-haired. The plane has aged as well, the plastic yellowed, the wiring faulty, the bolts weeping rust. Mystery #1 is solved. And Mystery #2 takes its place: what the hell happened on board this flight?

Soon the first responders will begin to notice strange things: watches stop ticking, lightbulbs sputter and go black, bad knees seize up, hair whitens, and liver spots rise from skin. Our caped crusader understands this as a phenomenon that causes aging, what turns out to be a virus. Mystery #3: what is its source and can it be stopped? And here is the moment—as a terrorist takes responsibility for the virus and the feds show up and quarantine the airport and Batman begins to age rapidly—when the stakes really deepen and the story kicks into gear.

Don't forget the most basic reason we read: to discover what happens next. Make certain your devotion to pretty sentences and flesh-and-blood characters and cityscapes and exquisitely crafted metaphors works in service of story, contributing to the momentum that will propel your readers forward.

If only Darren had chased down that man with the slicked-back hair and the aviator shades at Six Flags—and if only the punch line had turned out to be not a joke but a password—and if only the password had gained him access to an underground bar called the Dancing Tissue—and if only he had been escorted to a back room where the owner of that bar, a man with a mechanical leg and a mysterious tattoo on the back of his hand, poured him a whiskey and said, "I've been waiting for you, Darren. I've been waiting for you such a long time." If only his temporary blindness had led to a deepening mystery, then maybe his story would be worth telling.

If only someone had told him a joke with a much more valuable punch line. Q: What's the key to suspense? A: I'll tell you later.

Set Pieces
Staging the Iconic Scene

I didn't want the book, a coffee table book. *The Movie Book*—that was its title. It was a Christmas present, a big brick, maybe seven hundred pages, several old-growth forests pulped and processed. My grandmother said, "I thought you might like it," and I said, "Because I like movies," and she said, "Yes." The year before, it had been the *Quotationary*, because I liked words, and the year before that *The Book of Skulls*, because I liked skulls.

I don't understand coffee table books. You put them in the middle of your living room, fanned in a peacocky display, until they are too sun-faded or coffee-ringed, and then replace them with other continent-sized titles from the art museum or national park you just visited. You will never read them, because they are not meant to be read.

I did not read *The Movie Book*. I stuck it on a shelf and forgot about it. Until one day, years later, when absently fitting together LEGOs with my son, I dragged it down. It thumped onto the floor and split open to a still frame from *The Untouchables*. A baby carriage thunked down the stairs of the train station, while all around it gunfire flashed.

I turned the page and found Janet Leigh in the shower, her mouth a black hole of terror. A butcher knife plunged. Water needled her naked body.

I flipped to the next page. Julie Andrews spun on a mountaintop in *The Sound of Music*. Robert De Niro pulled a gun on his reflection in *Taxi Driver*. And on the next page and the next, Harrison Ford ran from a rolling boulder in *Raiders of the Lost Ark*, Dustin Hoffman stared hungrily as Mrs. Robinson sat on the edge of her bed and peeled a stocking from her leg. Every film had one shot, one defining image.

There is an acronym thrown around in screenwriting courses: MMM. Moments Make Movies. I like acronyms about as much as I like coffee table books, but this one is worth chewing on.

What do *you* remember when you think about the films splintered into your psyche? Consider *The Graduate* or *Gone with the Wind* or *Easy Rider* or *Annie Hall* or *The Empire Strikes Back* or *Casablanca* or *The Godfather* or *The Exorcist* or *Tootsie* or *Lawrence of Arabia* or *City Lights* or *Do the Right Thing* or *Seven Samurai* or *Jaws* or *Die Hard* or *The Wizard of Oz*. When you think of those films, there are probably several pivotal scenes—scenes of spectacle, scenes of horror or joy or absurdity or shock or profound empathy—that you cannot forget, ten minutes after you walk out of the theater, ten days, ten weeks, ten years. These are the moments that—in spite of the artful technique and the rock-solid structure and the flesh-and-blood characters—audiences will take with them to their grave. These moments will likely wind up in the trailer. And they are what you will gaspingly try to recount to your friends over beers in a bar.

Riffle through the catalog of literature and something similar will occur. Donna Tartt's *The Goldfinch* makes me think of the titular painting clawed from the rubble of the bomb-blasted Met, and her novel *The Secret History* instantly brings to mind the moment in the woods, on the trail, when Henry steps out of the trees and shoves Bunny off the ledge. When I think of Cormac McCarthy's *The Road*, I think of the house on the hill and what waits in its basement, and when I think of Mark Helprin's *Winter's Tale*, I think of the boat cracking through the frozen river and sending many black tributaries through the ice.

Most of the great movies, most of the great books seem to have three or four or five of those indelible moments, those moments that exist like dreams—or life, if only life could be so full.

Charles Baxter says that we write to make sense of the widowed images in our lives. Widowed images. Startling images. Haunting images. Iconic images. Indelible images. Whatever you want to call what ends up clogged in our imaginative filter. We don't always know why they're important, but for whatever reason, our mind won't release them.

I keep a giant corkboard next to my desk. Every day, when I sit down to write, my eyes skim across it. I've tacked to it pieces of paper, cocktail napkins, notecards. On them I have scribbled snippets of dialogue overhead at bars and diners and parties that I might later funnel into a character's mouth. Bits of trivia about mushrooms or volcanoes, some curiosity that might become a metaphor. And images. A gallery of images.

Some of these images I have cut from calendars, ripped from magazines or newspapers. Others are postcards mailed to me by friends or plucked from gift shop racks. Others I photographed. A coyote carcass in a dry canyon jeweled with flies. A shadow-soaked lithograph of Hansel and Gretel slinking through the woods. The long, rough, tangled bodies of blacksmiths in Goya's *The Forge*.

And some of these images—the widowed images—I have drawn from the deep well of memory.

When I was ten or eleven or twelve, my father demanded I follow him to the edge of our property, twenty-seven acres of big pines. He carried a rifle. A banshee wail rose from the forest. We followed the sound. Eventually we came to its source, a deer tangled in a barbed-wire fence like a bloodied marionette. He handed me the rifle. He wanted me to kill it, as if killing were as simple as tying a tie or fixing a carburetor. And I have toyed with variations on this moment in an essay, a short story, a novel.

My parents nearly bought a house built over a cave. The kitchen smelled like mushrooms and puddles. The Realtor led us through a door, down a steel staircase, and into a lava tube that stretched on for miles. My parents made an offer, but another family outbid them. A year later, the driveway opened and swallowed a truck. Soon afterward half the neighborhood knuckled upon itself. I never forgot the house and its dark, yawning staircase—and for years I kept a description of it on my corkboard until I found a place for it in a short story called "The Caves in Oregon."

When I was fourteen, my family camped at a lake walled in by high basalt cliffs. The water was so clear you could read the date on a quarter from twenty feet. I crushed my eyes into a pair of goggles and went for a swim and discovered a group of teenage girls gathering at the edge of a spur of basalt. They jumped into the lake, one by one, over and over, and I found, with the water so clear, I could see their bikinis torn away when they struck the surface. So I held my breath until my lungs burned and black dots swarmed my eyes and I watched them dive, their breasts bared, their bodies sleeved by white bubbles, as if they were boiling hot. Ten years later that became the opening of a short story called "Swans."

I did not know at the time why these moments mattered, but I knew they carried a current and I had to find a way to plug into the electricity.

That's what Brian De Palma, the director of *The Untouchables,* did when he shot the sequence in which the carriage tumbles down the staircase. He was directly channeling a scene in Sergei Eisenstein's 1925 film, *Battleship Potemkin.* And De Palma is not alone. Hitchcock echoed this scene in *Pyscho* and *Foreign Correspondent.* Francis Ford Coppola arranged a similar staircase scene in *The Godfather.* All of these directors, enraptured by the chaos and danger and vulnerability of that original moment, set out to make it their own.

I've done the same. In a six-page sequence in my novel *Red Moon,* at Pioneer Courthouse Square, in Portland, Oregon, during the annual Christmas tree lighting, a van veers off the street and through the crowd and crashes down the brick steps and into the amphitheater, yellow sparks spitting from its wheel wells. Carolers sing. A man dressed as Santa rings a silver bell. And the van, packed with plastic explosives, detonates in an orange flash that leaves the square a blackened crater with the Christmas tree at its center a towering cone of flame.

Try this out. Mine your past. Think of a place (say, a factory where your dad worked or a music camp you attended every summer through high school) or a time (like when you were dating a sociopath or slugging your way through chemotherapy). Three or four images will typically race to the front of your mind. You can hunt for these images, too. Keep your mind open, a notebook ready. That's what the novelist Claire Davis does. Every morning she walks her dog along the Snake River, and every morning she spots something she can use later at her desk: the way an osprey dives for a trout, the way the sun bursts over the mountains.

One Saturday night a few years ago, at Iowa State University, a student said "So long" to his friends, left a party, and vanished. Some said suicide and some said murder. The Smiley Face Killer appeared in more than a few headlines. More and more news vans rolled into town. Search parties scoured the woods and ditches and fields. Dogs bayed. During this time, Rick Bass visited the campus for a reading. On our way to the event, we paused at a window in the student union, overlooking the campus lake. The cops sawed holes in the ice. The dark water bubbled when the divers slipped beneath the surface. For a long minute, Rick and I watched in silence. Then he turned to me and said, "You gonna call it? This belong to you?" and I said, "How about let's race?"

We both wrote stories that borrowed from that moment. I bound together the image of the dark hole cut into the ice-scabbed lake with another image from that time. Every winter, in Ames, Iowa, crows appear. Clouds of them. Thousands of them. They blacken rooftops and leafless trees. They mutter and wheeze. They slick sidewalks with their shit. They dive and peck people who walk too close. To keep them away, the university has installed sound systems that every few minutes play recordings of crows being tortured. It is an awful sound. I wonder about the recording of it, the crows being electrocuted, waterboarded in a sound studio somewhere.

It was the convergence of those two moments that inspired a story called "The Cold Boy." And this is my standard process: reap the images and then divorce them from life; find a construct that feels more truthful and compelling than reality.

So I gather these moments, I tack them to my corkboard, I glance at them every day. Now and then two or three or four of them will spark and glow and align themselves into a constellation. The question is, where do they belong? And how will they best serve the story?

Perhaps you're familiar with the term *set piece*. I thought I was. For years I heard my film buff friends talking about set pieces—for years I read reviews talking about set pieces—and I thought it translated literally: *set pieces,* the pieces of a set. The sand and stucco of the Mos Eisley spaceport in *Star Wars*. The gray-walled prison in *The Shawshank Redemption*. That's what the stupid, misleading term *ought* to refer to, but doesn't. Set pieces are the moments I was referring to before, when the stakes are escalated, the staging carefully managed, the special effects sometimes expensive and flashy. Alfred Hitchcock refers to them as *crescendos,* a much better term, which implies a heightening, a swelling, a loudness that demands the audience lean forward.

Just as the special effects—sharks attacking or trains wrecking or robots fighting—ramp up in these set-piece moments, in literature, too, there is often an amplification of language. Consider this scene from Cormac McCarthy's *Blood Meridian:*

> A legion of horribles, hundreds in number, half naked or clad
> in costumes attic or biblical or wardrobed out of a fevered
> dream with the skins of animals and silk finery and pieces
> of uniform still tracked with the blood of prior owners, coats

of slain dragoons, frogged and braided cavalry jackets, one
in a stovepipe hat and one with an umbrella and one in white
stockings and a bloodstained weddingveil and some in head-
gear of cranefeathers or rawhide helmets that bore the horns
of bull or buffalo and one in a pigeontailed coat worn back-
wards and otherwise naked and one in the armor of a spanish
conquistador, the breastplate and pauldrons deeply dented
with old blows of mace or sabre done in another country by
men whose very bones were dust and many with their braids
spliced up with the hair of other beasts until they trailed upon
the ground and their horses' ears and tails worked with bits of
brightly colored cloth and one whose horse's whole head was
painted crimson red and all the horsemen's faces gaudy and
grotesque with daubings like a company of mounted clowns,
death hilarious, all howling in a barbarous tongue and riding
down upon them like a horde from a hell more horrible yet
than the brimstone land of christian reckoning, screeching
and yammering and clothed in smoke like those vaporous be-
ings in regions beyond right knowing where the eye wanders
and the lip jerks and drools.

    Oh my god, said the sergeant.

This moment is preceded by relatively calm language and relatively calm circumstances—descriptions of the men riding through
the heat and desert wastes. And then, as the attacking horde approaches, McCarthy goes off leash. The sentences grow wild and
expansive, matching the material. It's the equivalent of the quick
series of camera cuts and heightened music that we encounter in
Hitchcock's famous shower scene, a stylistic intensification that
casts a spotlight on the sequence.

Over and over again, writers have obeyed that common writing
maxim "Be specific." But they go too far and end up choking readers
with detail. So there should be an asterisk next to the command "Be

specific." Be specific when something is interesting. When something is interesting, you look at it longer. You prolong and amplify. These set pieces are the most interesting moments and so they demand a slowness, an elongation. Stretch out the physical beats.

Let's say you're writing a detective story, and let's say you've come to the diner scene, where the detective flirts with a thick-waisted waitress named Flo, meets up with a wild-haired, lazy-eyed source, and from him gets some critical piece of information—maybe a photo or an address—before ordering a black coffee and a Reuben sandwich.

Please, at this moment, spare us a fifteen-page description of the Reuben.

When you let the camera linger, when you crowd a scene with details, you are announcing that everything is important, and if you do this constantly, then you are also saying that everything is important, and when everything is important, nothing is important. There is a direct ratio between the length and the function of a scene. Save the attention to detail for the scenes that matter most. Like, say, a set piece. Like, say, the summit of your story, when the detective kicks down the door to the warehouse and cartwheels through it with guns blazing and kills the ninjas lying in wait and rescues the kidnapped boy duct-taped to the chair in the back corner.

Forget the Reuben. Focus on the ninjas.

Here is a moment that focuses on the ninjas, a scene from "The Chain" by Tobias Wolff:

Brian Gold was at the top of the hill when the dog attacked. A big black wolflike animal attached to a chain, it came flying off a back porch and tore through its yard into the park, moving easily in spite of the deep snow, making for Gold's daughter. He waited for the chain to pull the dog up short; the dog kept coming. Gold plunged down the hill, shouting as he went. Snow and wind deadened his voice. Anna's sled was almost at the bottom of the slope. Gold had raised the hood of her parka against the needling gusts, and he knew she couldn't hear him or see the dog racing toward her. He was conscious of the dog's speed and of his own dreamy progress, the weight of his gum boots, the clinging trap of crust beneath the new snow. His overcoat flapped at his knees. He screamed one last time as the dog made its lunge, and at that moment Anna flinched away and the dog caught her shoulder instead of her face. Gold was barely halfway down the hill, arms pumping, feet sliding in the boots. He seemed to be running in place, held at a fixed, unbridgeable distance as the dog dragged Anna backward off the sled, shaking her like a doll. Gold threw himself down the hill helplessly, then the distance vanished and he was there.

The sled was overturned, the snow churned up; the dog had marked this ground as its own. It still had Anna by the shoulder. Gold heard the rage boiling in its gut. He saw the tensed hindquarters and the flattened ears and the red gleam of gum under the wrinkled snout. Anna was on her back, her face bleached and blank, staring at the sky. She had never looked so small. Gold seized the chain and yanked at it, but could get no purchase in the snow. The dog only snarled more fiercely and started shaking Anna again. She didn't make a sound. Her silence made Gold go hollow and cold. He flung himself onto the dog and hooked his arm under its neck and pulled back hard. Still the dog wouldn't let go. Gold felt its heat and the profound rumble of its will. With his other hand he tried to pry the jaw loose. His gloves were slippery with drool; he couldn't get a good grip. Gold's mouth was next to the dog's ear. He said, "Let go, damn you," and then he took the ear between his teeth and bit down with everything he had. He heard a yelp and something cracked against his nose, knocking him backward. When he pushed himself up the dog was running for home, jerking its head from side to side, scattering flecks of blood on the snow.

This is the beginning of the story, the inciting incident, the trouble that sets off a chain reaction. The dog attacks the child and the man attacks the dog. The blood is in his mouth, and it infects him, and so many pages later someone is dead from a crowbar to the temple.

I can't help but come back to *The Untouchables* here and wonder if Wolff, like De Palma, was inspired by that stairway sequence from *Battleship Potemkin*. Instead of a baby pram tumbling down the stairs in a storm of gunfire, a girl on a sled slips down a hill as a wolflike animal snarls toward her. The paternal Kevin Costner character is replaced by Brian Gold, both trying to save an innocent (note: put a child in danger, earn your audience's attention—works every time). Look at the slow-motion qualities—the elongation of time—as the child descends and the dog races forward and Gold kicks through the clinging snow. The point of view belongs to Gold, but Wolff cheats the limitations of his perspective by getting us inside his daughter's head (she can't hear him since the wind is gusting and can't see him since her hood is pulled up) and even the dog's (the trampled-down snow indicates its territory). This is the equivalent of a swift succession of camera cuts. We have close-ups (the descriptions of the dog's muzzle and hindquarters) and we have medium shots angled from above (the description of his daughter never having appeared as small as she lies in the snow). De Palma and Wolff draw from the same bag of tricks.

The shower scene in *Psycho* lasts three minutes and contains fifty cuts. Imagine if that same kaleidoscopic style were used throughout the film. We'd puke in our popcorn out of dizziness and overstimulation. Hitchcock saves it for maximum impact. So, too, do McCarthy and Wolff strategically blast off the fireworks, topple the domino display.

Take a few workshops, read a few craft books on fiction writing or screenwriting, and you'll encounter various charts and diagrams that say pretty much the same thing about how stories are structured. The introductory exposition supplies us with setting and character. The inciting incident introduces trouble and interrupts the established habits of the world. The character fights his or her way through a gauntlet of obstacles and arrives, finally, at the high-stakes tournament, and, depending on the outcome, we are left with bluebirds and sunshine or bats and grave dust.

Indelible images almost always align with the introductory sequence and the climax. The most critical moments in your story (the initiation of the trouble and its resolution) are the most deserved. Think of Stephen King's *Carrie* and your mind instantly fractures the story into two moments: the young woman covered in menstrual blood at the opening and then in pig's blood at the climax, on both occasions surrounded by cruel laughter.

In a short story you may be reduced to one or two moments, but if you own more narrative real estate, as in a novel or memoir or film, you can potentially have more. Consider the faked orgasm in *When Harry Met Sally . . .* , the phone booth ravaged by gulls in *The Birds,* the dojo fight sequence in *The Matrix.* And consider the knife fight in McCarthy's *All the Pretty Horses,* the shadow-soaked exploration of Vlad's fortress in Elizabeth Kostova's *The Historian,* or the moment in Frank Herbert's *Dune* when Paul Atreides summons and rides a massive sandworm. All of these scenes jump-start the inevitable sag that weighs down the second act.

Break down that story you're writing by itemizing its set pieces. Carve away everything else, because your reader will forget nearly everything else, their experience ultimately defined by the crescendo. If it's a short story, do you have at least one set piece? If it's a novel, do you have at least four? And have you given them the necessary minutes of footage, the careful staging, the special-effects budget they deserve? This is what will launch your story from merely memorable to iconic.

There Will Be Blood
Writing Violence

You shut out the lights, crawl into bed, pull the sheets up to your neck, and try to settle into sleep. But you can't. Because of the noises that suddenly invade the night. The hardwood creaking. Pipes moaning in the walls. Cats howling in the backyard. The icemaker clattering cubes into its tray. Moments ago, when the house was filled with light, when you were watching television or surfing the Web, you were fine. But now, sitting up in bed, your heart thudding in your chest, you are convinced a knife-wielding maniac is creeping through the house. Because once the lights go out—once your vision is canceled—once one sense is shut off—the others heighten.

Filmmakers know the trick. This is why the camera pans away from the severed ear in *Reservoir Dogs*, leaving us with screams. This is why gunfire sounds after Roberto Benigni marches away from his son in *Life Is Beautiful*. This is why you listen to Leland Orser's hyperventilating confession of a rape/murder in *Seven*. The directors are trying to scare their audience, yes, but the fear and pain you experience are all the more unsettling because they are participatory. You share the experience as you invent it.

I. The Obscene

Writers, take note. If the text of your stories is occasionally written in red—you slice a wrist or scissor off a nose or run over a poodle—then you've no doubt been quizzed about representations of violence in your work. Authors have been asked such questions as long as stories have been told. There's no knowing what queries Greek tragedians fielded about the violence in their plays, but the great acts of classical brutality (Oedipus gouging his eyes out; Clytemnestra slitting her husband's throat) are never *portrayed* but rather *reported* by the characters or chorus—told but not shown. These days, *tell* is a bad word. But in the golden age of Athenian drama, telling was a celebrated technique. Acts of violence in Greek tragedy were rendered *ob skene* (literally "offstage"), from which comes the present-day word *obscene.*

In these times of excess, it's important to revive the discussion of obscenity, the art of restraint. The concern here is not with what is moral, or right, or proper, but rather with what is effective, asking how depictions of violence best serve a story.

The dark-hearted godmother of literary fiction, Flannery O'Connor, when discussing her use of violence in "A Good Man Is Hard to Find," has this to say:

> We hear many complaints about the prevalence of violence in modern fiction, and it is always assumed that this violence is a bad thing and meant to be an end in itself. With the serious writer, violence is never an end in itself. It is the extreme situation that best reveals what we are essentially, and I believe these are times when writers are more interested in what we are essentially than in the tenor of our daily lives. Violence is a force which can be used for good or evil, and among other things taken by it is the kingdom of heaven. But regardless of what can be taken by it, the man in the violent situation reveals those qualities least dispensable in his personality, those qualities which are all he will have to take into eternity with him.

O'Connor uses violence to unmask, to strip a character to his core. The Misfit from "A Good Man Is Hard to Find" is not "the man in the violent situation": he *is* that situation. He is the agent of violence that O'Connor uses to reveal her characters, to peel back their layers and expose what's beneath. He goes on to challenge every tenet of the grandmother's belief system as her family—son, daughter-in-law, granddaughter, and grandson—are led off-scene and into the woods to be executed. The ditch is the stage and the audience remains with the faithful sociopath and faithless old woman while they discuss, among other things, Christ. Pistol shots echo from woods that "gaped like a dark open mouth." The grandmother won't enter this forest, and neither will the reader, but the family members are marched off to be serially devoured. The effect is akin to a countdown, a bomb ticking. When the father is ushered away with the son, the reader thinks, *They'll kill the men, but surely not the women.* Until, of course, they very politely pull the mother to her feet and walk her away as well. The grandmother voices precisely what the reader is thinking: You wouldn't shoot a lady, would you? The Misfit can reply only that he'd hate to have to.

Interestingly, the shooting of the grandmother is not rendered obscene. And yet the reader doesn't exactly *see* it. O'Connor chooses here to tell the violence rather than to show it: "She reached out and touched him on the shoulder. The Misfit sprang back as if a snake had bitten him and shot her three times through the chest." O'Connor doesn't display the violence. Instead, she shows the results: "the grandmother who half sat and half lay in a puddle of blood with her legs crossed under her like a child's and her face smiling up at the cloudless sky." The carnage O'Connor reveals is a savage, zero-sum redemption, and the grandmother's reward for recognizing (re-cog-nizing = re-think-ing) the Misfit as "one of [her] own children" is tranquillity and peace: the Misfit's violence returns her to a posture of innocence, like a child's.

Now imagine that O'Connor hadn't led the family into the woods. Imagine if instead she had allowed the Misfit to execute them publicly, if she had detailed the father's skull opening up, the bits of brain decorating the grass. If the mother had clutched her boy, rocking his corpse and crying out even as blood filled her lungs. Or imagine that Joyce Carol Oates—who uses a similar technique at the end of "Where Are You Going, Where Have You Been?"—had taken us out of the house, into that car with the grinning pumpkin painted on it, up the driveway, and down the road to the field where young Connie would be held down, raped, and strangled to death.

The stories would not resonate as they do. Why? As the stories are written, they invite the audience backstage—into the dark—where imagination takes over and the reader becomes a kind of writer, inventing the violence, and in doing so the story becomes their own and they carry it with them like a red-veined tumor.

And the technique suits the purpose of their stories. O'Connor and Oates are both concerned with the ordinariness of evil. Bad guys don't necessarily wear a black mask and carry a red light saber, nor do they howl at the moon or sleep in dirt-filled coffins. The Misfit talks like a deranged philosophy professor, but otherwise his "hair was beginning to go gray and he wore silver-rimmed spectacles that gave him a scholarly look." In Oates's story, Arnold Friend has "shaggy black hair" and dresses like any other teenage boy: in "tight faded jeans stuffed into black, scuffed boots, a belt that pulled his waist in and showed how lean he was." The villains of their stories look like people you might pass in the cereal aisle at the grocery store. Evil is banal. And the point is emphasized through the use of the obscene: when the violence occurs offstage, the reader creates it and becomes a perpetrator. Goethe famously said, "There is no crime of which I do not deem myself capable," and O'Connor and Oates imply the same is true of us. You are a molester. I am a murderer. We have, each and every one of us, bodies in the basements of our minds.

Evil is more than ordinary to Cormac McCarthy—it is pervasive. In *Blood Meridian*, baby corpses hang from a tree like ornaments, scalps are shaved away from skulls, men and women, alive and dead, are raped. A head is lopped off with a single swing of a bowie knife. A blazing howitzer reduces a crowd of men to hamburger. McCarthy bathes in pools of gore and towels off with his pages. Which is why his use of the obscene (offstage violence), at the end of *Blood Meridian,* is so unexpected and powerful.

There are no heroes or villains in the novel—no lines in the sand except those made by the winding paths of snakes—but if we had to choose sides, the kid would be our protagonist, the judge his adversary. In the final pages, the kid thinks he has escaped the endless slaughter of the desert, thinks he has escaped the wrath of judgment, but then one night he wanders behind a saloon and opens the outhouse door. "The judge was seated upon the closet. He was naked and he rose up smiling and gathered him in his arms against his immense and terrible flesh and shot the wooden barlatch home behind him."

McCarthy cuts away from the scene. McCarthy—who up to this point has shown us everything, every knife jab and rifle shot and arterial spray—gives us nothing. There is no greater surprise in the novel. What happens in the outhouse? Not even the two men can tell us, when they stumble their way to the jakes and hammer at the door and eventually yank it open, except to say, "Good God almighty":

> What is it?
> He didn't answer. He stepped past the other and went back up the walk. The other man stood looking after him. Then he opened the door and looked in.

McCarthy's outhouse stands in for O'Connor's forest: they are the dark mouths that every writer should consider using: their holes hold shadows and in that sudden darkness, who knows what terror and wretchedness you and your readers are capable of?

II. Gorenography

We're all guilty of it at one time or another. Excess. Recklessness. Dangerous indulgence. Driven by the same impulse that compels us, when we spot a sign that reads *Wet Paint,* to reach out a hand for a touch, delighting in the smear, bringing a finger to our nose for a sniff, to our tongue for a taste.

Especially when the paint is red.

So many of my students—mostly young men egged on by I don't know what: Xbox, Hollywood, Axe body spray?—prolong suffering and splash buckets of blood across their stories without principle and with peculiar malice and glee. I call this "gorenography" and it strikes me as hollow, excessive, masturbatory. Of course, violence must sometimes occur onstage instead of off—but when you force your audience to stare into the abyss, consider the following.

III. Two for Flinching

Here is something I often scribble in the margins of student papers: "Sounds like writing." Meaning, for one reason or another—usually the student is trying too hard, choking their sentences with purple prose—I fall out of the story. I am aware of myself as a reader, aware that I hold in my hands ink and paper instead of flesh and blood.

The same thing happens when I watch a Michael Bay movie. I am aware of the film as a film. In the darkened theater, during a scene where Las Vegas is ripped apart by Transformers, I might turn to the person next to me and whisper, "What great special effects." I'm not weeping or laughing or even gripping my armrests after experiencing a spike of adrenaline—I'm simply marveling at the way computers can create illusions: a casino exploding, a robot folding itself into the shape of a semi truck.

That's what the work of Chuck Palahniuk and Bret Easton Ellis occasionally feels like: a special kind of CGI meant to sour your stomach. When Patrick Bateman, the narrator of *American Psycho*, describes his extracurricular activities as a serial killer over and over, beat by beat, the knives, the scissors, the chain saws, the rat tunneling through the cavity of a victim still alive . . .

Or when Palahniuk, in his short story "Guts," describes, at length, anal injuries people have suffered, including a passage about a boy enjoying and then trying to escape the suck of a pool filter only to discover that his lower intestine has been turned inside out and he is trapped underwater by a translucent rope speckled with peas and corn and a bright orange vitamin pill . . .

Their flamboyant style aestheticizes the mayhem, as if the authors love what we are meant to despise. They linger on the violence, wallow in the gore, celebrate it to such a degree that I can almost see them smirking, hear them snickering, and they essentially become that kid we all went to middle school with—Cody: big ears, buzz cut, braces—who would fake a punch, and then, when you startled, would screech, "Two for flinching," and sock you twice in the shoulder. Don't be a Cody. Nobody liked him.

IV. Earning Violence

Often, when I judge the length and vividness of a bullet-pocked, blood-soaked scene compared to another scene, the story appears unbalanced.

That moment when the husband realizes that his wife wants a divorce, that she has been hammering the headboard with the UPS man for the past six months? It gets a paragraph. But the passage detailing the way the cuckolded husband then maims, shoots, splashes with gasoline, and finally burns the UPS man to ashes goes on for two pages.

Of course, I ask the student if that scene should exist at all—if he thinks the reader will listen only if the drama is so top-volume—but regardless of that, I point out how lopsided the story is, how the majority of it is devoted to broken bones, shattered teeth, intestines yanked from a carved-out belly like party streamers. I know so little about these people—the husband, the wife, the UPS man with his brown shorts—that I couldn't care less whether or not the marriage dissolves, whether or not one of them gets chopped up into itty-bitty pieces.

Meaning the violence is unearned. You must *earn* violence. Build up the kindling and pipe in the oxygen before you strike the match. Because it serves an important function in a story, as a transformative device, a catalyst for change. The bullet that whizzes from the jungle and kills Ted Lavender, described over and over again in Tim O'Brien's *The Things They Carried*, forces Lt. Jimmy Cross to get his head out of the clouds and focus on the war, to finally lead his men, to keep them safe. The ax murder of the pawnbroker in Dostoyevsky's *Crime and Punishment* transforms Raskolnikov into a paranoid obsessive who suspects everyone and ends up giving away all the money he has stolen, as though to purge himself of any guilt. Sethe runs a saw blade across her own child's neck in Toni Morrison's *Beloved*, and the death ghosts its way through the novel (literally and metaphorically), haunting her, so that she is shunned by her community and her relationship with Paul D is tested.

Violence is not the answer, but a variable in a long, complicated equation.

V. The Menace of the Mind

In *Frenzy*, Alfred Hitchcock's penultimate film, there is a scene in which Bob Rusk (played by Barry Foster) escorts a barmaid to his apartment. His voice is casual—as they walk through a warehouse, along a sidewalk, into his building, up the stairs—but his eyes are sharp, his expression forbidding. When he unlocks the door and motions her in, we understand that he means to kill her.

Curiously, rather than follow them into the apartment, the camera remains in the hallway. The door slams shut, the bolt is driven home. A faint struggle is heard. But the camera doesn't linger. Instead it slowly descends the stairwell, spiraling downward, exiting to the street, where the noise of traffic and conversation takes over.

Hitchcock knows the imagination has a darker power than anything he can show us. By closing the door, he opens our mind to the very worst, a technique he uses over and over—even at his most excessive.

Consider the murder of Janet Leigh in *Psycho,* one of the most famous scenes in film history and one of the most definitive scenes of violence in all of storytelling, shot over seven days and featuring seventy-seven camera angles and fifty cuts. Almost every shot is a close-up, each of them flashing on-screen for the briefest moment, giving us a shutter-speed collage of horror. A screaming mouth. An outstretched hand. A bulging eye. Knife, knife, *knife.* You imagine you see the murder, but not once during these three minutes do we actually witness skin penetrated, an artery severed, a blade catching against a rib, what we would have observed if the scene were shown continuously or at a wider angle.

Hitchcock described this as "transferring the menace from the screen into the mind of the audience." And isn't that your goal? To make an audience feel? So that they are not bystanders but accomplices? Hitchcock makes this possible by supplying minute particulars, never showing us everything, only glimpses that anchor the moment and allow us to fill in the rest of the nightmare.

VI. Violence and the Emotional Arc

In most stories, there is a narrative arc and an emotional arc. The narrative arc is what happens, one thing leading to another, a series of scenes that crash together and lead to some sort of rousing climax, such as when Dorothy travels to Oz and has a bunch of happy, crappy adventures.

The emotional arc is how the character transforms as a result of the narrative. So Dorothy, after her adventure, goes from being an antsy dreamer—staring at the horizon while singing "Somewhere over the Rainbow"—to a realist, someone who finally appreciates what she has, where she's from, tapping those ruby slippers together and saying, "There's no place like home."

In the story "A Distant Episode" by Paul Bowles, a linguist—known only as the Professor—travels to Morocco to meet up with a colleague and study the dialects of the country. He treats the locals as inferiors, showing off his intellect, insulting them with his cultural aloofness, trying to appease them with money. He is, in short, a pompous asshole. One thing leads to another, and in his search for some novelty camel-udder boxes, he ends up getting kidnapped by a group known as the Reguibat, who beat him badly and then cut off his tongue:

> The man looked at him dispassionately in the gray morning light. With one hand he pinched together the Professor's nostrils. When the Professor opened his mouth to breathe, the man swiftly seized his tongue and pulled on it with all his might. The Professor was gagging and catching his breath; he did not see what was happening. He could not distinguish the pain of the brutal yanking from that of the sharp knife. Then there was an endless choking and spitting that went on automatically, as though he were scarcely a part of it. The word "operation" kept going through his mind; it calmed his terror somewhat as he sank back into darkness.

This is where everything shifts. The point of view up to this point belonged to the Professor, the language and the perspective informed by his arrogance and intelligence. No longer. His voice fades and he becomes a background character as the Reguibat make him into an amusement. They dress him in a brightly girdled costume and string tin cans around him and demand that he dance and grunt after feasts, to everyone's merriment.

What a perfect place to direct the violence, to focus our attention: on the tongue, the very organ that got him into this mess. Its excision is transformative, almost atoning, a shift in the narrative and a shift in character. For a year, he eats, he defecates, he dances when bidden. He has lost all sense of self and becomes the primitive he once perceived the locals to be.

When I read about the knife sliding across his tongue, I am not flinching as a reader—I am flinching as an accomplice in the story, emotionally moved, at once horrified, disgusted, and weirdly satisfied that the Professor has received his comeuppance. The moment is not there to titillate. Because I am emotionally invested, I do not see the author's hand—I see only the hand of the Reguibat gripping the knife—and the passage electrifies (rather than electrocutes) my senses.

VII. Choreography

There's a reason why the violence in Cormac McCarthy's novels so disturbs and unsettles us (while always feeling appropriate to the story), and it has everything to do with *credibility*. For examples, you could turn to any of McCarthy's books (or to just about any page of *Child of God*), but a glance at the climax of the masterful novel *All the Pretty Horses* serves nicely. Here our hero, John Grady Cole, locked in a Mexican prison, must defend himself against the knife-wielding inmate hired to murder him—opportunities for gainful employment in mid-twentieth-century Mexican prisons being, of course, somewhat scarce. It is the first time we witness our cowboy protagonist fighting for his life, and McCarthy choreographs the scene with all the absorption of a ballet teacher or Kali instructor. As readers, we are acutely aware of his opponents—both spatially and temporally. So often, when beginning writers attempt to portray a melee, the result is mere confusion: readers have little sense of where the combatants are standing, of how they are moving and striking, of the pacing, the timing. McCarthy records all of this with a director's eye.

The stage: a lunchroom filled with prisoners who at the first sign of conflict back up against the wall.

The props: two switchblades, two steel lunch trays, a table, and a bench.

The actors: a young Mexican assassin simply called "the *cuchillero*" (Spanish for "cutler," or, more colloquially, "knife man") and a sixteen-year-old Texas farm boy.

As the audience, we watch each slash and stab and feint and parry, the assassin's blade like "a cold steel newt seeking out the warmth within him," conscious as well of our hero's other sensory experiences: the quiet of the room and the clang of the lunch trays, the smell of his would-be murderer, the taste of blood in his mouth, the feel of it as he touches his shirt with a hand that comes away "sticky." The choreography of movement and the attention to sensory detail grant the scene remarkable credibility. We read with a quickening pulse as John Grady is cut repeatedly, as he appears to give up, sits down, and slumps against the wall. When the young assassin seizes John Grady's hair and pulls back his head to cut his throat, John Grady plunges his knife into the assassin's heart and breaks off the blade inside him. McCarthy understands that fight choreography has its own narrative logic and presents (if done well) its own mini-drama. Like Muhammad Ali fighting George Foreman, John Grady manages to rope-a-dope his opponent, and readers enjoy the exhilaration of victory even as they feel the sickening pain of his wounds, physical and psychological.

VIII. Moral Instructiveness

There is a scene in the film *12 Years a Slave*. A scene I can't get out of my head. A scene I did not want to watch. In it, Solomon Northup (played by Chiwetel Ejiofor) is left to hang all day. His neck is noosed, but his feet still touch the ground, barely. The prolonged shot is grueling to endure. Because there is no cut, there is no relief, only awkwardness and pain made all the more uncomfortable due to the wide-shot reveal of the other slaves ignoring him, going about their daily chores, helpless to help him.

There are no flashy special effects. No manipulative music (aside from an initial throbbing of a baritone sax that gives way to cicadas). Just the lingering gaze. No sound outside the creaking of the rope and the straining of his breath and the squishing of his tiptoes as he renegotiates his balance in the mud and tries to keep from strangling to death.

It's good that this struggle did not take place offscreen. It's good that I was made uncomfortable. It's good that I was forced to painfully watch. We must witness the horror because the horror happened. I'm talking about individual and generalized truths. *12 Years a Slave* was based on a memoir, but even if it were a novel it would be true. The hatefulness and suffering endured by Solomon—embodied so beautifully and miserably in this scene—speak to the larger catastrophe of slavery. The author (whether a writer or a filmmaker) is a servant of memory and must make certain the reader never forgets, must hold up a mirror to truths we would rather not acknowledge.

The sparseness and the unblinking gaze of that scene remind me of a passage from Harry Crews's essay "Fathers, Sons, Blood." In the opening scene, he awakes to his wife screaming and his children yammering. He overhears snippets of conversation—"Patrick . . ." ". . . in the pool . . ." ". . . get him out." And with that, Crews throws back the covers and sprints down the hall and out the front door to the pool two doors down:

> As I went through the open gate of the high fence surrounding the pool, I saw my son face down in the water at the deep end, his blond hair wafting about his head the only movement. I got him out, pinched his nose and put my mouth on his mouth. But from the first breath, it didn't work. I thought he had swallowed his tongue. I checked it and he had not.
>
> I struggled to breathe for him on the way to the emergency room. But the pulse in his carotid artery had stopped under my fingers long before we got there, and he was dead. That morning, at breakfast with his mother, he'd had cereal. The doctor told me that in the panic of drowning, he had thrown up and then sucked it back again. My effort to breathe for him had not worked, nor could it have. His air passages were blocked. In a little more than a month, September fourth, he would have been four years old.

He does not look away. To look away would make things easier on us. He wants to inflict a wound on us. He wants us to feel and know his loss. We are not told about his aching heart or his mind stricken black with grief. We are shown a boy floating facedown in a pool, his blond hair wafting in the water. We are shown a father's mouth over his son's, trying to give breath. And all this time his tone remains straightforward, his language simple, every description brief. He does not need to hyper-stylize the content: material like this needs the volume turned down, not up. And god, it hurts.

Violence is a powerful and simple way to embody conflict. Violence is redemptive. Violence is transformative. But more than that, violence is a necessary reflection of this world and our wounded lives.

A quick survey of this morning's headlines reveals the following. An officer was killed in a shooting in a Baltimore nightclub. The remains of an exotic dancer were discovered outside of Las Vegas. A dozen decapitated bodies were left outside a shopping center in Acapulco. A male model killed and castrated a Portuguese journalist in a New York hotel. And at a political meet-and-greet at a grocery store in Tucson, Arizona, a man opened fire. A congresswoman was shot in the head. Five others were killed, including a nine-year-old girl. This is the world we live in. You don't have to look that far to find horror. And your job as a writer, no matter how uncomfortable, is to occasionally but *responsibly* shine a lamp lit with blood into those dark corners of human existence.

Making the Extraordinary Ordinary

I was not allowed to see Tim Burton's *Batman* when it was released—my parents were sticklers about the PG-13 rating, and I was ten at the time. Maybe because it was forbidden, I became obsessed with the film. I wore a *Batman* T-shirt, hung a *Batman* poster above my bed, scribbled *Batman* doodles in the margins of my notebooks, bought *Batman* comic books, figurines, trading cards. I can't remember how many cards there were altogether—let's say one hundred—but I collected them all. They showed stills from the film—Michael Keaton at the wheel of the Batmobile, Jack Nicholson splattered on the pavement after his long fall from the bell tower—and I would lay them out on the floor of my room, arranging and rearranging them, trying to figure out their order so that I might play an imaginary version of the film in my head, already a young novelist toying with character and structure.

The film, when I finally rented it and popped it into my VCR, disappointed me. Because my version of the story was better. I had spent so much time with the characters, dreaming about them for months on end, that they felt more real to me than some of my schoolmates did. One of the central questions in *Batman* is this: is Bruce Wayne playing the monster or is the monster playing Bruce Wayne? This is a question Frank Miller and Christopher Nolan much more successfully addressed. Tim Burton's film (and the painful succession of sequels that came before *Batman Begins*) made the

Dark Knight so cartoonish that the question was irrelevant. Burton was enamored with the gritty nightmare of Gotham, the whiz-bang awesomeness of the Batmobile, and was careless with characterization. So I didn't believe.

I was around the same age as the young Bruce Wayne when his parents are gunned down. Imagining the loss of my own parents, the love and security they provided, devastated me, the ultimate horror. As strange as this seems in retrospect, I would cry over my trading cards—projecting myself into that blood-soaked alley—and then, when I didn't have any more tears, I would wipe the dampness from my face and get mad. Darkly so. I had too much empathy; it was a superpower (as a budding writer) and a disability (as a functional human being). I descended into an emotional abyss where I could imagine perfectly the hell I would bring to the criminals of Gotham City. My mind warped into a nihilistic revenge-machine. I was only a child, but after dreaming my way darkly through Gotham, the movie felt comparatively silly. Because it had no heart.

I went through another severe projective experience when I read Stephen King's *The Gunslinger,* the first in the Dark Tower series. I was thirteen—and about to change schools, about to leap from seventh to eighth grade. Thirteen is the worst year of anybody's life, but I had an especially awful run. In trouble for fighting. In trouble for vandalism. In trouble for stealing. In trouble for grades. I remember my mother crying and running upstairs when I was suspended. I remember my father ripping up my report card and hurling the pieces across the room like the saddest sort of confetti, not saying a word, just staring at me with hooded eyes. They made the decision to pull me out, to put me in a different school with smaller classes and stricter discipline.

I lived in the country, in the nowhereland of sage flats and alfalfa fields that stretch between Bend and Redmond, Oregon. Reading was an antidote to the isolation. Of course the plot grabbed me by my throat (which was pretty scrawny back then), but Roland was the real reason the book impacted me so profoundly. Roland of Gilead, the lead character, the titular gunslinger. This might seem ridiculous—but remember that I was thirteen, when everything is ridiculous, and I was leaving one school and entering another, forty miles away. I can remember my parents telling me the new school would change me—that change was good; I needed to change—and I agreed with them. I felt like a pitiful smear of human waste and was actively thinking, Who do I want to be?

Roland answered that question. He seemed like the ultimate man. He lived by a knight's code of honor. He withstood pain with gritted teeth. He was disciplined, knowledgeable, strong. He was in pursuit of something important—his presence in the world mattered. He was never the one to start a fight but always the one left standing. He rarely spoke, but when he did, his words were wise and impactful. Silence, I came to understand, was knowing when to shut up. I became deeply reticent that summer—and the silence lasted until I graduated from high school.

Some might have mistaken my silence for shyness, but it was something else: I was a strategist, holding back, judging every word, every action, trying to decide its merit. You know those kids with the wwjd wristbands? I should have had a special one made—what would roland do? I understand that this sounds horribly corny, but it's true, and back then it mattered to me more than anything in the world. My grades improved. I became painfully serious, my face absent of expression. Sometimes I would lie in bed and chide myself for something I had said or done that seemed to me ill-becoming, and it was as though, in the shadows shifting on my ceiling, the shape of the gunslinger was taking form.

I've read *The Gunslinger* more often than any other book. I'm still that teenage boy when I crack it open. But I'm a writer, too, and I especially love the hybrid quality of the narrative—it's a western, it's a fantasy, it's a horror novel, and it brings to mind, too, legends of knights rattling their swords in battle, following a chivalrous code. The world King created—a postapocalyptic world, a sorcerous world—enchanted me, but it was Roland who ultimately moved me, transformed me. The story had heart. It was a leathery, sand-dusted heart, but a heart nonetheless. Roland was the reason King was writing a novel, whereas Gotham was the reason Tim Burton was making a movie, which resulted in something heartless: all style, no substance.

Most beginning writers, when they first get caught up in a thrilling idea, fetishize the whoa-dude-ain't-this-coolness of it all. Let's call this tendency giganticism. They focus on the ninja with X-ray vision who will save the world—or the river zombies with steak knives for teeth who will destroy the world—or whatever spectacular hoo-ha they have dreamed up. And in doing so they neglect character.

You have probably encountered this quote by Chekov: "In descriptions of Nature one must seize on small details, grouping them so that when the reader closes his eyes he gets a picture. For instance, you'll have a moonlit night if you write that on the mill dam a piece of glass from a broken bottle glittered like a bright little star, and that the black shadow of a dog or a wolf rolled past like a ball."

This good advice typically illustrates the importance of avoiding abstraction and anchoring a narrative with details. You're not writing about the moon; you're writing about the moonlight glinting off shards of glass. In a wedding scene, you're not sweeping over the congregation tucked into their pews and staring at the happy couple at the pulpit; you're zooming in on the flower girl vigorously picking her nose, the scar-tissue-pink gum stuck to the bridesmaid's high heel, the kaleidoscopic light of the stained-glass window. In a scene set in a forest, you're not merely describing the sweep of evergreens or the darkness beneath their boughs; you're homing in on the shed elk antler lying in the very center of a bear-grass meadow, the half-buried, rust-specked, bullet-ridden Folgers can used for target practice, the nest a crow made from the flaxen hair of a girl's corpse.

But the advice can translate to human particulars as well. Don't neglect them in favor of the "big idea." Your vampire apocalypse, your clone invasion, your school of wizardry and witchcraft. Matters of the heart make your world worth occupying. Especially when it comes to high-concept storytelling. This, I'm guessing, is one of the unarticulated reasons so many professors forbid so-called genre fiction in their workshops. The story about Planet Doom is often so enamored with its hook, its weirdness, its world-building charms, that the focus diffuses, abstracted beyond the particulars of human existence. Over breakfast, we'll skim an article about some country on the other side of the world ripping itself to shreds, but really we're more concerned about scraping the last bit of peanut butter from the jar. We need the everyday to balance out the astonishing. Make the extraordinary ordinary.

That's what George Saunders does in so much of his fiction. Consider his short story "Sea Oak." The narrator works at a strip club called Joysticks. He lives in a squalid rental in a rough neighborhood with his sister, Min, their cousin, Jade, and his aunt Bernie, who has worked her whole life as a clerk in a chain drugstore. Bernie dies—but soon after the burial, the police call to report that the grave has been disturbed, and the coffin is empty. The narrator comes home from work and finds the door wide open, his sisters cowering on the couch, and Bernie's body slumped in the rocking chair. But this is no ordinary zombie story, as Bernie's gut-busting monologue proves:

> "You, mister," Bernie says to me, "are going to start showing your cock. You'll show it and show it. You go up to a lady, if she wants to see it, if she'll pay to see it, I'll make a thumbprint on the forehead. You see the thumbprint, you ask. I'll try to get you five a day, at twenty bucks a pop. So a hundred

bucks a day. Seven hundred a week. And that's cash, so no taxes. No withholding. See? That's the beauty of it."

She's got dirt in her hair and dirt in her teeth and her hair is a mess and her tongue when it darts out to lick her lips is black.

"You, Jade," she says. "Tomorrow you start work. Andersen Labels, Fifth and Rivera. Dress up when you go. Wear something nice. Show a little leg. And don't chomp your gum. Ask for Len. At the end of the month, we take the money you made and the cock money and get a new place. Someplace safe. That's part one of Phase One. You, Min. You baby-sit. Plus you quit smoking. Plus you learn how to cook. No more food out of cans. We gotta eat right to look our best. Because I am getting me so many lovers. Maybe you kids don't know this but I died a freaking virgin. No babies, no lovers. Nothing went in, nothing came out. Ha ha! Dry as a bone, completely wasted, this pretty little thing God gave me between my legs. Well I am going to have lovers now, you fucks! Like in the movies, big shoulders and all, and a summer house, and nice trips, and in the morning in my room a big vase of flowers, and I'm going to get my nipples hard standing in the breeze from the ocean, eating shrimp from a cup, you sons of bitches, while my lover watches me from the veranda, his big shoulders shining, all hard for me, that's one damn thing I will guarantee you kids! Ha ha! You think I'm joking? I ain't freaking joking. I never got nothing! My life was shit! I was never even up in a freaking plane. But that was that life and this is this life. My new life. Cover me up now! With a blanket. I need my beauty rest. Tell anyone I'm here, you all die. Plus they die. Whoever you tell, they die. I kill them with my mind. I can do that. I am very freaking strong now. I got powers!"

It's more than hilarious—it's tragic. She has returned from the dead because she never really lived. Saunders reinvents genre by giving it a beating heart. And he normalizes the weirdness by giving her a pitiable desire we can all relate to. Would the story be just as effective if it were told as realism? Some might say so. But fantasy allows us truths that might otherwise be unavailable. Normally our reflection means little except as a way to check our teeth, to smear on makeup, but before a warped mirror we pause, studying ourselves with awe and care, struck by a new way of seeing.

That's how I feel when I read Karen Russell. Her story "St. Lucy's Home for Girls Raised by Wolves" might be about werewolves, but really it's about adolescence. The hormonal surges that make us into wild things, id-driven lunatics. And that's how I feel when reading Aimee Bender. Her story "Marzipan" might be about a man who wakes up with a hole in his stomach, but it's really about grief. "One week after his father died," it opens, "my father woke up with a hole in his stomach. It wasn't a small hole, some kind of mild break in the skin, it was a hole the size of a soccer ball and it went all the way through. You could now see behind him like he was an enlarged peephole." Grief is about an aching absence and here the metaphor is made literal. The weirdness somehow clarifies our everyday struggles.

I read a story in an undergrad workshop—more than a decade ago—that I still think about now and then. It concerned a magic pipe. Not the kind you smoke. Just a short length of steel pipe. Point the pipe at something and it vanishes. The narrator—lazy, a bit of a moron—happens upon the pipe one day, and it changes his life. He doesn't use the pipe, as you might expect, to attack the White House or even to blip out of existence some nemesis who works at Papa John's. Instead he uses it to clean up the dog poop from his yard. And the empty beer cans and crumpled Cheetos bags from his living room. The author doesn't fetishize the weirdness; he normalizes it, shaping a story about a small, sad man that has stayed with me all these years.

Kelly Link makes a similar move in "Origin Story." At a diner in a small town, the middle-aged waitresses can levitate, but they use their superpower only occasionally throughout their shifts to reduce the risk of varicose veins. And Nick Hornby does the same in *Otherwise Pandemonium*. The title story of the collection is narrated by a teenage boy who picks up a secondhand VCR from a junk shop to tape the NBA playoffs. When he accidentally fast-forwards past the game, he discovers that the VCR has recorded not only yesterday's events but today's as well, and tomorrow's, and beyond. He can watch next week's sitcom, next month's news. What he finds disturbs him. Political tension on a global stage. An outbreak of war. And then static. The world is coming to an end. What does he do with this knowledge? He uses it to get laid. Because he's been lusting after a girl named Martha. About her, he has this to say: "a) She's hot; b) but hot in a not-slutty way." They play in the same "dumb jazz orchestra thing." The interesting part of the story is not that the world ends. The interesting part of the story—and the most truthful, endearing, and weird part of the story—is about how they end up having sex. He shows her the magic VCR and tells her that he doesn't want to die a virgin. In these circumstances, "at least sex is something that's achievable."

Saunders and Hornby use this strategy as well: everyday narrators who use everyday language. "Oh, man" and "tortured genius-style dude" mellow the extreme material, making it that much more likely that we'll buy it, like a lobster roll, or accept it, like a bloodstained, diamond-encrusted dagger wrapped up in the funny pages. A colloquial tone and prosaic content can be the gateway to plausibility.

But not always. Consider the stylistic tactics of Mark Helprin and Téa Obreht. Their language exalts, enchants, reads like an incantation, sorcerously lyrical. They are writing fairy tales and fables ruled by whimsy. Even in a whimsical story like "A Very Old Man with Enormous Wings"—where the language is hyper-lyrical—Gabriel García Márquez still tries to bring the fantastic down to earth. We know what we're in for when we come across sentences like these, in the first paragraph: "The world had been sad since Tuesday. Sea and sky were a single ash-gray thing and the sands of the beach, which on March nights glimmered like powdered light, had become a stew of mud and rotten shellfish." This is a land of long ago and far away. But look at the way García Márquez describes the old man who appears out of nowhere, seemingly dropped from the sky into the mud in the corner of the courtyard. He is dressed like a "ragpicker" with "buzzard wings" and "only a few faded hairs left on his bald skull." We expect winged men to be angelic, muscled and white-robed and blonde-haired and backlit by radiant light, but García Márquez plays against our expectations: this figure is far from heavenly. They call him an "angel," yes, but they also wonder if he is a Norwegian or a sailor, a "castaway from some foreign ship wrecked by the storm." And he is not exalted, as we would expect, but persecuted. He performs no miracles. He cowers pitifully. They cage him, prod him, pick his feathers, throw stones at him, burn his side with a branding iron. And in this way García Márquez not only makes the fantastic accessible but captures the human tendency to fear whatever is different and the desire to label, define, control.

Anyone attracted to fairy tales and fables should check out the stories and criticism of Kate Bernheimer. I'll condense some of her thoughts here by saying that the fairy tale normalizes magic. If a baby turns into a pig, or a wolf speaks in a pleasing baritone, or a star descends from the sky and changes into an elderly woman with three wishes to spare, the characters do not question the illogic of the circumstances but freely accept that the surreal is real. Rarely does someone say "This can't be happening" in a Karen Russell story, a Kevin Brockmeier story, an Aimee Bender or a Matt Bell story.

Neil Gaiman's *The Ocean at the End of the Lane* makes for an interesting case study. Because Gaiman's adult narrator is unreliable—he admits to chasms in his memory—and because he is describing his adventures as a fanciful seven-year-old who spends his days lost in books, the reader can effortlessly accept the extraordinary made ordinary. Whether it is real or the wild dreams of childhood doesn't matter so much. Because to a child the jungle gym *is* a pirate ship, the shadow in the closet *is* a monster, the pennies in the belly of the piggy bank *are* gold. Imagination is reality.

As a writer, there are two ways you can go about this:

Give in to whimsy. Let the imagination run free. Werewolves attend boarding school (as in Russell's "St. Lucy's Home for Girls Raised by Wolves"); a black obelisk descends to Earth (Brockmeier's "The Ceiling").

Alternatively, you can try to persuade the reader that magic is perfectly reasonable. I did this in my novel *Red Moon,* researching animal-borne pathogens like those that cause mad cow disease and chronic wasting disease, creating a slippery science, a physical analogue to the werewolf myth in the hopes of creating a believable horror. Patrick Rothfuss, whose fantasy novels rival those of George R. R. Martin, spends a great deal of time explaining his magic system. There is such particularity to his spells and potions, all of them so convincingly described that the reader feels enchantment is within reach. Sometimes I feel like there is almost a mathematical relationship between the weirdness of certain material and how precise you must be with everything else, which is maybe why so many sci-fi and fantasy novels run long, as the writers know they must fatten the story with exposition that will make the dragons or robots more plausible.

I struggled with this balance between whimsy and logic when reading *The Ocean at the End of the Lane.* It feels rather curmudgeonly to say this, but I'm not sure you can have both. Gaiman talks about "Dark Matter, the material of the universe that makes up everything that must be there but we cannot find," and riffs his way into a kind of quantum physics school of magic. This aligns nicely with the Hempstocks' ability to snip out pieces of time, channel energy, remember the Big Bang. But then something more whimsical will pop up, as when a character mentions that Cousin Japeth "went off to fight in the

Mouse Wars." That sort of silliness feels like a slight to the more substantial world-building Gaiman has achieved. When you create a logic system, a contract with your reader, I suppose you could say, you need to stick with it. When Gaiman waffles, the spell breaks.

As an experiment, try changing one thing. Just one. This is our world except for _____. Maybe gravity is increasing incrementally. Maybe it won't stop raining. Maybe the sap from a certain maple tree makes a syrupy love potion. Maybe Stonehenge is a portal to the twelfth century. Maybe death is a red-tape bureaucracy serviced by bored, black-suited agents. You might find this constraint limiting, but this *one* thing will change a thousand things. Think of it as a stone thrown into a pond, rippling outward. If you do this, if you limit the change, and if you closely monitor the effects of it, then through this limitation and its accompanying logic system, you increase the likelihood that your audience will willingly suspend its disbelief. Some have built their careers on this practice. Others use it as a starting point.

Tim O'Brien, in "How to Tell a True War Story," writes about making the reader believe. "Often the crazy stuff is true and the normal stuff isn't, because the normal stuff is necessary to make you believe the truly incredible craziness." This applies to war stories, yes, but also to troll stories, to ghost stories and superhero stories and detective stories. The normal stuff is necessary. With this in mind, go ahead: cast your own spells, build your own worlds, but consider carefully the many normalizing strategies of make-believe or we won't be willing to follow you to long ago and far away.

Designing Suspense

I. Worst-Case Scenarios

I'm always talking about mapmaking, blueprinting, planning out a story before beginning it. People seem to find this either upsetting—"You take the fun out of writing!"—or perplexing—"How do you graph a story? What is a beat sheet? When do certain actions or emotional gateways need to occur?"

Yes, they're right: nothing *needs* to happen, but some things commonly do. There are no rules, but there are "rules," certain foundational truths you should understand and master before experimenting beyond them or flouting them altogether. Know these "rules" before you break them. Literary writers will often dismiss anything that even vaguely resembles a prescription, which strikes me as both cavalier and negligent.

Consider this: Picasso trained in realism before he shattered our way of seeing. Patricia Smith can rock a sonnet or villanelle as well as experiment with free verse. Seth MacFarlane is an accomplished classical pianist who can also write crass, wandering comedic ballads. Can you say the same? Can you write something that is scene-driven and as tightly fitted as a LEGO castle and then turn around and write something masterfully nonlinear that artfully employs summary? Or are you exclusively "artful" because it's easier to excuse your sloppiness as purposeful? "Oh, the fact that nothing happened in my story? That's because I was trying to capture the nothingness of the modern condition." Uh-huh. Sure. Good luck. Beckett's already got that covered.

Me, I'm a fan of the woodworker who can carve a badass eagle out of driftwood *and* build a solid-ass rocking chair.

Books and movies share many characteristics, but because film structure is usually tidier, the screen is sometimes easier to study when it comes to tracking and comprehending the standard beats of a narrative. Humans all have the same basic design—femur here, liver there—and yet we're all such a bunch of different goonies. Despite a shared anatomical composition, people are as different from each other as Cher and Muhammad Ali. In the same way, screenplays—which are far more rigid in their structure than novels—share the same design, and yet the results are as varied as *The Princess Bride* and *The Terminator, Caddyshack,* and *Gone with the Wind.*

Characters need a higher-order goal. This determines the course of the narrative. Find the treasure; win the big game; stop the zombie virus from spreading. Most writers seem to get this, but when I ask them to figure out their ending before they begin, they waffle or panic. This is the target your arrow will hasten toward. Every paragraph, every chapter will be written in pursuit of it. And even if you do know your ending, that leaves a lot of intimidating white space to fill up.

Here is another, less common juncture to consider: the worst-case scenario. If you know your higher-order goal, and if you know your characters' weaknesses, the calculus isn't complicated.

What does Indiana Jones want in *Raiders of the Lost Ark*? The ark, of course. That's what the men in the suits charge him with finding. His central goal is its acquisition. Now, what is Indiana Jones afraid of, besides losing the ark to Belloq and the Nazis? Snakes. We know this from the beginning, when he climbs into the single-engine hydroplane and discovers a python curled up beneath his seat.

What, then, is his worst-case scenario? The ark's secret location is a chamber swarming with thousands of asps. Jones and Sallah enter through the ceiling, throwing down a rope, descending into the dark. With a torch Jones waves away the spitting snakes. He is sweating, whimpering, wide-eyed with fear. The ark gives off a golden glow when they lift it from a sarcophagus and then hoist it through the hole in the ceiling. It is then, when the ark vanishes from sight, that the Nazis appear, smiling down on Jones and sealing him inside.

He has lost the ark—and he might lose his life to the thing he fears more than a firing squad: "Snakes. Why did it have to be snakes?" Worst-case scenario: check.

Angela Carter does something similar in her short story "The Bloody Chamber," a lush, disturbing revisionist fairy tale. On the very first page, we discover what our character fears—not a snake, but an empty purse. She has married a Marquis, the "richest man in France," abandoning her single mother and banishing "the spectre of poverty from its habitual place at our meagre table." Her mother presses her, worries over her, asks her if this is really what she wants. Her daughter assures her it is, even as she worries about the face of her husband: "And sometimes that face, in stillness when he listened to me playing, with the heavy eyelids folded over eyes that always disturbed me by their absolute absence of light, seemed to me like a mask, as if his real face, the face that truly reflected all the life he had led in the world before he met me, before, even, I was born, as though that face lay underneath this mask."

His engagement ring is a "bad luck" opal. Everywhere she goes in the castle, there are "funereal lilies." He makes her wear a "choker" made of rubies "bright as arterial blood," and kisses it before he kisses her lips the first time he beds her (they do not "make love"; that's for certain). Oh yeah, and I forgot to mention: he was married three times previously, to women who presumably died but whose bodies were never discovered. Despite all this, early on she hopes that he might love her and care—to join his "beautiful gallery of women"—despite her being a "poor widow's child with my mouse-coloured hair that still bore the kinks of the plaits from which it had so recently been freed, my bony hips, my nervous, pianist's fingers."

Her greed—her desire for a pampered life—has led her to this doomed marriage. The worst-case scenario is no surprise: she discovers a room, down a cobwebbed hallway in the castle, full of instruments of torture, including an iron maiden in which resides the fresh corpse of his previous wife.

Our narrator has ignored her mother's warnings—and she has ignored her heart—and though the Marquis's attention at first makes her feel special, beautiful, she comes to realize it is her innocence and vulnerability he finds so appealing. That is why he calls her "baby." That is why he laughs with relish when she startles at opening a slim volume full of sexual illustrations. That is why he delights when he strips her naked before a dozen mirrors and she trembles in response.

At first she believes he has saved her life, when in fact the marriage has doomed her. She recognizes this as the juncture of the second and third acts, after he discovers she has entered his bloody chamber—and before she and the blind piano tuner will attempt to escape the husband's wrath. Ultimately it is her mother who saves her. Astride a horse, wielding her late husband's revolver, firing it into the Marquis's forehead with the same accuracy she used to dispose of a tiger long ago (all of this set up on the first page).

With lovely symmetry, the very person our narrator hoped to escape in the beginning saves her in the end. The opening anticipates the ending. And the worst-case scenario is not only the hinge between them—it's also the very thing that gives the story resonance. As in life, it's difficult to appreciate success without first experiencing failure.

Here's an exercise for you. Start with reality. Come up with a moment when you really, really wanted something. Could be you wanted to land a job or could be you wanted to quit a job. Could be you wanted a divorce or a proposal. Could be you wanted a cancer-free future after a nasty diagnosis. Recall that moment. Then inject it with a healthy dose of imagination. What is the worst-case scenario for this character? (Not you, not anymore, since now we're dealing with somebody in a story.)

So let's say a couple really wants a kid. They try for two years. Tirelessly hurling themselves into bed, studying their diet, giving up alcohol, paying attention to ovulation cycles—but it never happens. Then they throw down a big wad of cash for in vitro fertilization—and still, sadly, nothing. They make the decision to adopt.

Worst-case scenario? The kid is a nightmare. Maybe they adopt a nine-year-old from Russia who is malnourished and abused, so he has physical and emotional issues. He trashes the house, bites anyone who gets near him, pisses his way through five mattresses. All they wanted was a child. They thought it would consummate their love, make their marriage complete. Now that they have a child, their relationship is on the skids. They decide to give the kid up.

If you're a short-story writer, maybe you leave us soon after this, closing with some ambiguous darkness. Don't do this—it's too Hallmarky—but imagine our story ending with the boy looking pathetically pale and small in the rear window of a car as it pulls away. You'd write some better version of that because people who read short stories love endings that make them want to gargle with Drano or nosedive off a skyscraper.

But if you're writing a novel or a memoir or a screenplay, your audience will usually hope for a gladder, luckier closure. Indiana Jones will escape the chamber of snakes and retrieve the ark. Bilbo Baggins will overcome Smaug the terrible and return the Lonely Mountain to the dwarves and hike home to the Shire. The Bad News Bears or the Mighty Ducks will overcome their star player's injury and will rack up (barely) enough points to win, because even though they suck, they have heart!

And maybe this couple will end up keeping the child after all (after some scenario, heart-bruised with sentiment, that cements the possibility of their happy hand-holding togetherness).

This moment almost always comes, in long-form narratives, at the juncture of the second and third acts. Call it the rock-bottom moment, the dark night of the soul, whatever. Your character will be ready to give up—before they rally and enter the final act, swinging. If you know the worst-case scenario, then you know its placement, so you know one of the brighter stars in the narrative constellation.

From here, if you're outlining, it's simply a matter of reverse engineering.

You've heard before that a story is about a series of battles, with the biggest battle of all waiting for us at the end. But here's another way to think about it: as a series of failures leading toward the biggest failure of all (from which redemption is possible and success appreciated).

The shark starts killing people in *Jaws*. Chief Brody wants to keep the island safe. What's the first failure? He tries to shut the beaches down. The mayor opposes him. It's tourist season, after all. So Brody climbs the lifeguard tower and glasses the water with his binoculars, hoping to watch over everyone, warn them out of the waves if he spots a threat. He does. And everyone crashes onto the beach in open-mouthed panic. But he was wrong—it isn't the shark—it's bluefish, just a school of bluefish. Now he looks like a fool. So he pulls back from his nannying of the beachgoers. What happens then? A kid gets killed. What happens then? Boats take to the ocean, hoping to kill the monster, and yes, they catch a shark, but no, the bite marks don't match up. One thing leads to the next thing, everything a failure, until Brody is compelled to charter a vessel (despite his fear of the water) and hunt down the fish himself (and even then he fails and fails and fails better).

In screenwriting, a *beat* refers to an action and a reaction. I've just listed off a chain of beats linked by failure. Check out a more microscopic version of this in Lydia Davis's "The Outing":

An outburst of anger near the road, a refusal to speak on the path, a silence in the pine woods, a silence across the old railroad bridge, an attempt to be friendly in the water, a refusal to end the argument on the flat stones, a cry of anger on the steep bank of dirt, a weeping among the bushes.

I don't know whether to call this a short story or a poem, but it reads to me like a beat sheet, a narrative stripped down to its essentials. And because it is short (and literary), it ends with sad ambiguity, the equivalent of our Russian orphan's pale face in the car window.

Whether we're talking about Steven Spielberg or Lydia Davis, the same narrative rhythm applies: action, reaction, action, reaction, action, reaction, many of these scenarios erupting from the character's botched response to an incident (and the botched responses to all trouble that erupts thereafter). In this way we are hurried toward the final showdown. This is the power of *negative thinking*, an alternate way to regulate the ripple effect of a casual narrative.

Samurai are said to have spent hours every day imagining all the things that might go wrong in battle. A feint, a duck, a broken sword, a severed limb, someone tripping, someone screaming, someone attacking from behind. Then they would try to imagine a way out of the situation. This helped them stay cool when they fought. They knew how to respond to muddy terrain, a gouged eye, a five-on-one fight, because they had already experienced such obstacles a thousand times over. Know your worst-case scenario and you know the way of the samurai—a clear-eyed method of negotiating the gauntlet of storytelling trouble.

II. The Dance of the Flaming Chain Saws

Every now and then a book catches fire. Everyone is reading it, talking about it: *The Da Vinci Code, The Kite Runner, Life of Pi, Fifty Shades of Grey, Wild*. For a good few years, Stieg Larsson's *The Girl with the*

Dragon Tattoo was that book. I'd wander through an airport and spot hundreds of copies on every concourse, the fluorescent-yellow cover glowing in everyone's hands.

I wanted to understand its popularity—and I wanted to figure out how a book 672 pages long could seem so compulsively readable. So I read it in a flash, and then I read it again, this time with a pen and a yellow legal tablet, outlining the structure. I paid particular attention to trouble. Emotional, physical, financial, familial, and professional trouble. Mikael Blomkvist's reputation has been slandered—he's experiencing legal and financial issues—he's sleeping with a married woman—he's on the rocks with his daughter—he's battling isolation and the elements on a cold northern island—he's chasing down a labyrinthine mystery—his life is in danger—and on and on. His point of view is balanced out by Lisbeth Salander's. She is weighed down by troubles of her own and eventually their story lines thread together when they become lovers, partners.

I began to color-code the major problems the characters faced— in blue, black, red, green, yellow, pink, purple—and to track page numbers. Larsson would introduce a blue problem on page 25, return to it on 78, 169, 240, 381, and so on, each time ratcheting up the tension and complicating things further. Interspersed with the blue problems were red problems, pink problems, a kaleidoscope of trouble, ever-changing.

I have come to call these flaming chain saws. Your success as a storyteller has to do with your ability to juggle them. Every time the flaming chain saws pass through your hands, they gain speed, become more perilous, until at last they are extinguished.

The more characters you have, the bigger the book, the more flaming chain saws. Let's say the average novel has seven. One might be romantic (somebody chasing somebody for a date, a kiss, a relationship), another might be financial or professional (somebody getting fired or hunting for a promotion or hoping to keep their bakery afloat), another familial (a divorce is imminent; a child is getting into trouble at school), another physical (somebody can't stop eating or blows out a knee or gets diagnosed with cancer).

I wrote four failed novels before I finally figured out the long form. I cannot list off all the reasons these manuscripts turned to dust in my hands, but one of my major errors was this: I treated chapters like short stories, introducing and resolving trouble in fifteen pages. I guess my arms got tired. I guess I wasn't much of a juggler. I guess my flaming chain saws ran out of gas too quickly.

The containment, the stand-aloneness of my chapters, gave my books a stop-start quality that destroyed any sense of momentum. Take a look at any novel—how about *The Island of Dr. Moreau* by H. G. Wells—and you can see how the chapters build toward a point of tension and then cut away. Chapter one ends with our sick, starved narrator floating in a dingy after eight days at sea! Chapter two ends with the mystery of what waits on the deck of the schooner that rescues him! Chapter three ends with an argument between the doctor and the captain! Chapter four ends with the appearance of the doctor's hideously deformed assistant (who gives our narrator nightmares)! Chapter five ends with the captain throwing our narrator off the ship! If you think about it, isn't there always an exclamation mark hidden in the white space? It's the equivalent of the commercial break.

I'm not the first to say that this is the golden era of television. HBO, Showtime, AMC, and FX are all airing episodes that don't stand alone, but build a narrative throughout the season, cumulative stories that track like novels. Study their scripts and you'll shortcut your way to an outline, the equivalent of my legal-tablet study of *The Girl with the Dragon Tattoo*. Oftentimes, after watching an episode of *The Sopranos, The Wire, Game of Thrones, Mad Men, Breaking Bad,* or *Orange Is the New Black,* I'll read the script and slash through it with highlighters, feather it with sticky notes, paying particular attention to the way the showrunners manage trouble—through each act—through each episode—through each season.

When sketching out your early plans for a book or when revising the draft of a manuscript, do the same. Identify the flaming chain saws and make sure your hands and pages are busy with the constant rotating threat of them.

III. Mapmaking

Sometimes I follow my own advice. Let me tour you through an architectural study of one of my novels. In *The Dead Lands,* my post-apocalyptic reimagining of the Lewis and Clark saga, a super flu and a nuclear Armageddon have made a husk of the world. The Sanctuary—the fortified remains of downtown St. Louis—believes itself the last outpost of America, the flag carrying a single star. Fearmongering leaders keep the citizens cowed and safe, but a rebellion is stirring. Then one day a rider (my Sacagawea character) appears out of the wastelands, sharing news of water, civilization, the promise of the West. And so a band of rebels, led by Lewis Meriwether and Mina Clark, head off with the hope of expanding their infant nation.

I've always been interested in fishbowl scenarios. Stephen King plays with them often—in *Under the Dome, The Mist, The Langoliers, Rita Hayworth and the Shawshank Redemption, The Green Mile.* An invisible dome appears over a town, a mist full of monsters oozes across the world, a caged door rattles shut and a key turns. The characters are trapped, the pressure is on, and certain traits end up magnified by the stress of the situation. Lust, love, courage, murderous rage, loyalty, religious fanaticism—they all heighten and come crashing together in one wild social experiment.

This is how I was thinking of the Sanctuary. As a prison like Shawshank. One the characters are born into and must escape if they're ever really going to transcend the limitations of their existence, to grow up as individuals and as a country.

I also love quest stories. *The Road, The Hobbit, Heart of Darkness, True Grit.* But they're extremely difficult to write well. Because the straight line—get the character from here to there, with various obstacles to overcome—often results in an episodic quality that feels redundant and doesn't contribute to momentum.

In *The Dead Lands*, I was trying to compound two narrative designs I admire, to create something complicated and hopefully new. Some of my characters are on a quest, moving from point A to point B. But by flashing back and forth between the Sanctuary and the journey west, I'm able to enhance suspense (by leaving the reader hanging with every chapter break) and to contrast the terrors and hopes of two very different worlds. The more time we spend in the Sanctuary, the more we understand why the perilous escape from it is so necessary.

Because I have two stories threaded together, I have two higher-order goals, which means I also have two worst-case scenarios. The Lewis and Clark expedition wants to make it to the Pacific (a concrete destination) and in doing so reunite the states (an abstract hope). When they arrive in Oregon, they discover a rising darkness. The very place they hoped would save the world may in fact ruin what little remains of it. Not only that, but the expedition has fallen apart due to betrayals among its members. Unity, on two different levels, has splintered. All is lost.

Then there is the Sanctuary, where unrest stirs and the administration punishes any who question its imperialistic politics. The wells are breaking down. The water is running out. And two young lovers (their relationship a secret) are doing their best to overthrow the mayor and bring about change. I'm afraid I had to kill one of them (and crush the rebellion). I had to make it seem as though the mayor had won—worst-case scenario—in order for him to ultimately lose.

The flaming chain saws are legion. The danger of radiation cycles in and out of the novel (not just its poisoning effects, but its mutating influence). So does heat (specifically as it relates to the lack of water, which affects the people of the Sanctuary and Lewis and Clark on their quest). Love is found and love is lost. Some struggle with depression and others with rage. Familial loyalties are tested. Friends are deceived. My Sacagawea character has a terrible secret— which I reveal in parcels—that clues us in to the horror that awaits them out west. The expedition is pursued by an enemy from the Sanctuary whose loyalties supposedly shift, but there remains the question of whether they can trust him. Lewis struggles with addiction. Clark struggles with the terrible knowledge that she killed Lewis's ailing mother in order to get him to agree to leave (a secret that, of course, will eventually be exposed). I could go on. Every one of these elements I keep in a rotation, alternating the tension, making you wonder about one while I jerk your attention toward another.

There's something horribly manipulative about all of this. Here I am—talking analytically about worst-case scenarios and juggling trouble, mapping out the embattled terrain of novels and comics and screenplays—but when you get right down to it, I'm suggesting that the best way to mess with the head of your reader is to strategize the delivery of bad news.

Don't Look Back

I've never kept a diary. I don't flip through old photo albums. I haven't watched a minute of the hundreds of hours of video I've shot of my kids ripping open presents, racing through sprinklers. When we ready the car for a trip, I stalk through the house several times and interrogate my wife, asking, "What about this? What about this? What about this?," making certain we've remembered everything, so that when we're blasting along the freeway, an hour from home, we don't have to turn around.

Maybe this is why I get so irritated by backstory.

When you're a beginner, stick to the rules. Listen to the sensei when he tells you to achieve some mastery of karate before you start trying to kick down doors, or you're going to shatter your ankle and fall mewling to the floor. So when my students ask me how much backstory they're permitted to include in a story, I say, "How about none?"

None is a good start. Because it's so often unnecessary. A reader intuits the history of a character by observing them acting in the present. If you were, say, at a house party full of teenagers—hosted by a fifty-year-old still wearing his high school letterman's jacket—you would no doubt draw your own conclusions independently as you observed his dyed hair, whitened teeth, the way he sidles up to a girl who could be his daughter and persists in dragging her onto the dance floor even when she tells him no. He drinks so much he can't count the change he needs for the pizza delivery. He throws his arms around a bull-necked young man and persists in telling a damp-eyed, slurred-voice story about going to the state championship years ago. You don't need the author leaning in to tell you this guy lives in a state of prolonged adolescence, that he was once the king of his high school, the captain of the football team, and though he headed off to college with big plans, he couldn't take being a little fish in a big pond and ended up dropping out sophomore year to return home and work for his pops at the used-car dealership. Now he buys the teenagers beer in order to relive those glory years, to get a taste of the power he has lost. If you explain all of this, you are no different than the man himself, howling with laughter at some locker-room joke from twenty years ago, forcing the reader to look at his glorified past when they understand perfectly well the sad ugliness of his present.

This is the wrong move for two reasons. First, because the impulse to explain will insult the reader. That's their job—part of the pleasure of reading a story is inference, filling in the blanks and becoming a participant in the narrative, a coauthor. As a beginner, you've had more training in reading than you've had in writing—and so, succumbing to insecurity, you announce, you explicate, making as a writer those inferences you're used to making as a reader.

"The first thing you'll probably want to know is where I was born, and what my lousy childhood was like, and how my parents were occupied and all before they had me, and all that David Copperfield kind of crap . . ." You probably recognize this quote from J. D. Salinger's *The Catcher in the Rye*. Try not to forget how it concludes: ". . . but I don't feel like going into it, if you want to know the truth. In the first place, that stuff bores me."

Second, stories are about forward movement, and if you turn to backstory, you have effectively yanked the gearshift into reverse. The story is no longer rushing forward—it's sliding back.

At one time or another you've probably heard a writing instructor talk about the A-B-D-C-E structure of a story, an acronym for Action-Background-Development-Conflict-Ending. You open with some sort of gripping action—say, a giant squid with an ink bazooka fighting a grizzly bear in a submarine—and then you take us back in time to contextualize the trouble before revving up the engine again. I understand the formula—I know it's used often and effectively. My problem, more often than not, comes when writers get stuck on B.

Sometimes the background goes on and on and on until we forget about the dramatic present—in which case the writer needs to yield to the possibility that the past should be *made* present. The history *is* the story. I'm thinking of a piece I workshopped that described a woman standing on the roof of a building, smoking a cigarette, staring out at a nighttime city, thinking about her mother. This went on for two pages, and then the story slid back in time and toured us through her whirlwind childhood. By the end, we returned to the roof, but the backstory was not only wildly more interesting than the frame, it took up nine of the fourteen pages.

And sometimes the writer feels compelled to constantly remind us of the past, as if trapped in an A-B vortex. A character is drinking tea at the breakfast table when she notices a fissure in the cup— the tea is leaking from it, snaking hotly down her wrist—and just like that the present dissolves into a moment, years before, when her husband slammed shut the dishwasher to get her attention and shattered half the glassware inside. Cut to the next scene: she's in the shower, and as the room fills with steam she recalls the first time they hurriedly made love, beside a pool at the Hampton Inn in Lawrence, Kansas. This is what I call the *Scooby-Doo* trick. The screen goes wavy—a harp strums three times—and we're transported back in time. Not only does it feel artificial, not only does it continuously yank the narrative into rewind, but in this case, it typically points to a stagnant story, a character given too much time to muse and ponder their cavernous navel.

I will say, by way of compromise, that this predilection for back-story works better in first person than in third. The first-person narrator *should* be more free-associative, more apt to digress. That's how our minds are wired. That's how we speak. Easily distracted, we loop away from the story we started. Unless you're writing in close third—so close that the narrative bends around the character's voice, the synaptic firing of their mind—the author is in control and that makes the backstory feel especially inauthentic and contrived.

There are ways to slip backstory into a narrative and not detract from momentum, such as slipping history into the predicate of the sentence. Maybe your character hates her overbearing mother. She has done everything she can to distance herself from the woman—moving thousands of miles away, changing her voice to shake the Ukrainian accent she inherited, even telling friends her mother died of cancer years ago—but still she is haunted by reminders. They share the same bulging knees, weak chin, brittle fingernails. And maybe, in a passage, you might write, "When she drove, she hunched into the wheel of the car and peered over its rim, muttering curses at the traffic around her, this white truck driven by an idiot, that minivan driven by a moron, furious at the whole world for doing her some injustice, with the same white-knuckled grip and scowl her mother wore when driving her pink Cadillac down country roads and gravel driveways, trying to sell bright, cakey Mary Kay makeup to anyone who would invite her in for lemonade and a makeover." The back-story fills the adverbial slot—coloring the way the girl drives—and then the next sentence comes along and we're back in the present, tearing along the freeway.

That's what Annie Proulx does in her story "The Half-Skinned Steer." An old grouch named Mero is driving his Cadillac to Wyoming—to attend his brother's funeral (he was killed by a "waspy emu")—when he is pulled over by a cop with a mustache. The officer asks the old man to take it easy, not drive so fast. "You're a little polecat, aren't you, [Mero] said, staring at the ticket, at the pathetic handwriting, but the mustache was a mile gone, peeling through the traffic as Mero had peeled out of the ranch road that long time ago, squinting through the abraded windshield." In the adverbial slot we learn about his propulsive exit from the state, so many years ago, so we understand better how much he has changed since then and how difficult and bewildering it is for him to return.

In "A Temporary Matter," Jhumpa Lahiri writes, "She wore a navy blue poplin raincoat over gray sweatpants and white sneakers, looking, at thirty-three, like the type of woman she'd once claimed she would never resemble." Here is a brief flash of backstory—again contained in the adverbial slot—that illustrates a larger truth about the story: things have not turned out as the couple planned. They are at odds with each other and the present.

If used sparingly—and strategically—backstory *can* have a propulsive force. Consider the embedded scene. You already know that when reaching a section break or concluding a chapter, it is wise to cut away at a moment of heightened action, to send your reader into white space wondering what happens next. Rather than immediately satisfying the reader's curiosity, you can heighten suspense by leaping forward in time and continuing to withhold information.

Let's say your character, Burt, runs a coffee shop and one day a girl walks in off the street. She appears homeless: her clothes are secondhand, her backpack is greasy and bulging. She waits in line and when it's her turn, she simply stands there, trembling. Burt says, "What would you like? A hot chocolate maybe?" But she's not there for a drink. She's there to identify Burt as her father. End scene.

You are following several points of view in this novel, so when you cut to a new chapter, it's a new perspective. We're left hanging, wondering what the hell happened in the coffee shop. When we finally return to Burt, he's at home with his very pregnant wife. Their marriage is on the rocks. They're expecting their first child. And now he has to tell her about the girl in the coffee shop. He won't know for sure until he takes a paternity test, but the girl's story checks out: her mother is an addict he had a fling with a decade ago. You see—the scene is rolling forward with great tension, and the tension is made that much worse because we still don't know what happened in the coffee shop. Now you deliver the backstory. Burt laughs at the girl, asks her if this is her idea of a joke, a way to score a free snack, and only when she begins to cry does he notice their eyes are the same shade of blue-green and he walks around the counter and ushers her to a table with a cookie and a lemonade and spends the next twenty minutes speaking to her in a hushed voice and finally promises that if what she says is true, he will take care of her. The backstory, sandwiched into the scene with his wife, compounds the pressure.

William Gay plays around with a similar move in his haunting short story "The Paperhanger," which begins with the line "The vanishing of the doctor's wife's child in broad daylight was an event so cataclysmic that it forever divided time into the then and the now, the before and the after." How she vanished, we don't know, not until the conclusion of the story, when Gay reveals that the wall-paper hanger, when working in the doctor's house, reached out and snapped the child's neck and tucked her into his toolbox and left. By carving away that essential piece of information, Gay creates dreadful suspense: the reader hunts the whole story for that miss-ing puzzle piece, not really wanting to find it. When the backstory is finally supplied—alongside the seduction of the mother by the paperhanger—it has a poisoning effect unequaled in fiction.

Here's another take on the move, this one from Kent Haruf's *Benediction*. Rob Lyle is the new preacher in town. He lost his previous post, in Denver, after supporting another preacher who came out as a homosexual, and he remains outspoken in his be-liefs at the Community Church in Holt. "Afterward it wasn't clear what Lyle expected the sermon to accomplish. But he wasn't even half-finished when some of the congregation, men mostly, hurry-ing their wives and children with them, began to rise up from their pews and glare at him and walk out of the church." We are teased with trouble. From there we slide back in time and walk through the service from its beginning: the call to worship, the first hymn, the reading of the Bible text, and the offering to follow. Eventually, and with dread, the sermon comes. Lyle begins by discussing the Sermon on the Mount and from there questions Jesus's teachings and launches into a politically heated discussion of the war raging overseas. By the time he finishes, the church is nearly empty. This chronological rearrangement—flashing forward, sliding back—creates an impetus, an energy the scene would not possess otherwise.

I know, I know: you don't agree with me and you can think of ten thousand awesome examples of backstory, like the staggered reveal of a couple's troubled relationship in Andrea Barrett's "The Behavior of Hawkweeds" or the back-and-forth tug-of-war that takes place in Edward P. Jones's *The Known World* or even the two-minute montage sequence in Pixar's *Up*. Keep in mind that I often make loud, growly pronouncements about things. "Do this," I tell my students. "But *never* do that." My hope is, maybe a week or a month or a year later, they will be seated at the computer, composing a story, and when they violate one of my rules, the screen will open up and my face will emerge and say, "Doooon't doooo thaaaat." Think of it as a more aggressive version of Microsoft Word's AutoCorrect, the squiggly green underline replaced by a bellowing spectator. The truth, of course, is that if you're good enough, you can do anything. William Gay can use backstory, William Trevor can violate point of view mid-scene, Alice Munro can write a short story that takes place over several decades, not because they're ignorant of the risk, but because their writing is so good it transcends the violation.

In other words, never use backstory—except when it works.

Modulation
The Art of the Reversal

I feel about novels as I feel about tattoos: you need to think about them for a good long time before you commit to the ink. Otherwise, in your drunken rush, you might end up with the equivalent of Yosemite Sam on your ass. I typically brainstorm for an entire year before I touch the keyboard. The previous owner of my house was a hobby photographer and he used my office closet as a darkroom. It's fitting, I suppose, given my disposition, that I use the darkroom as a playground for ideas, my nightmare factory. At any given moment I might be toying with five different story concepts, and I assign each a different section of the darkroom. I tack up articles torn from newspapers and magazines, interviews I've conducted, photos, paintings, anything that might inform the story. Every morning, before I sit down to hammer, I spend a little time under the red light, drinking my coffee and scribbling down a few more thoughts.

I rip a long sheet of paper off my kids' Melissa & Doug art easel, and I tape it up and begin sketching out characters. I mean this literally. I often draw them. Eyes that squint even with no sun. A nose as sharp as a quill. A mossy beard that tumbles down a chest. Then I'll begin to construct a kind of Wikipedia entry, figuring out their histories. Things get really interesting when I figure out what my characters want. Because when I know what they *want*, I can set obstacles in the way of that desire, and these are the first stirrings of plot.

A thread reaches across the sheet of paper—a story thread—and then another and then another, one for each character, often a tangle of them since I tend toward ensemble narratives. All of this is written in pencil, of course, because so many things will change. And then, on top of it all, I begin to map out what looks like a cardiogram or the lines made by a seismograph, what I call a suspense-o-meter.

This registers the peaks and valleys of the narrative, the high-volume action sequences and the low-volume moments of repose, both necessary. By blueprinting this, I can step back and study the story as a whole. I'll see that I have a meditative scene (maybe a walk in the woods) followed by a scene in which the characters hash something out (maybe over dinner), and I'll recognize the narrative lag. Or I'll see four action sequences set one right behind the other—exploding helicopter, exploding car, exploding train, exploding elephant—and I'll recognize that my reader will grow numb to the pyrotechnics unless I spread them out. So I move scenes around, strategizing their placement as part of the larger orchestration of emotion.

A cardiograph, a seismograph, a suspense-o-meter, a sound-board. However you want to think about balance, modulation, expansion and contraction, the variation of style and content so that you might best manipulate your reader into feeling.

I'm bad about favorites. I have so many of them. If you ask me for a favorite food, I might say steak or pizza or pancakes or chicken tikka masala or Culver's Deluxe Butterburger or the #57 at the Thai restaurant down the road. If you ask me for a favorite movie, depending on my mood I might say *The Godfather* or I might say *The Empire Strikes Back;* I might say *Rocky* or I might say *Rocky IV.* I will probably say *Jaws* (a rare example of a film adaptation that's superior to the novel). I could teach *any* craft lesson, *everything* about the art of storytelling, by picking apart *Jaws.* I'll spare you that rant, but I will gush about my favorite scene from the film.

After a long day on the water, the men—Quint (Robert Shaw), Brody (Roy Scheider), Hooper (Richard Dreyfuss)—have retired to the belly of the boat. In the dim light, they're drinking whiskey and trading scar stories. One came from a moray eel. Another came from a thresher shark. Another came from an arm-wrestling contest in a San Francisco bar. Hooper points to his chest and makes a crack about how Mary Ellen Moffat broke his heart. They're laughing, pounding the table, pouring and toasting more whiskey—until Brody asks, "What about that one?"

He's talking about the scar on Quint's forearm, once a tattoo. Quint puts a hand over it, as if to muffle the question. "I got that removed," he says.

But the men press him—and he unleashes one of the great monologues in film history, revealing that he was onboard the USS *Indianapolis*:

Japanese submarine slammed two torpedoes into our side, Chief. It was coming back from the island of Tinian to Leyte, just delivered the bomb. The Hiroshima bomb. Eleven hundred men went into the water. Vessel went down in twelve minutes. Didn't see the first shark for about a half an hour. Tiger. Thirteen-footer. You know how you know that when you're in the water, Chief? You tell by looking from the dorsal to the tail. What we didn't know . . . was our bomb mission had been so secret, no distress signal had been sent. They didn't even list us overdue for a week. Very first light, Chief. The sharks come cruising. So we formed ourselves into tight groups. You know it's . . . kind of like old squares in battle, like you see on a calendar, like the Battle of Waterloo. And the idea was, the shark comes to the nearest man, and that man, he'd start pounding and hollering and screaming, and sometimes the shark would go away. Sometimes he wouldn't go away. Sometimes that shark, he looks right into you. Right into your eyes. You know the thing about a shark, he's got . . . lifeless eyes, black eyes, like a doll's eyes. When he comes at you, doesn't seem to be living. Until he bites you, and those black eyes roll over white. And then—ah, then you hear that terrible high-pitch screaming, and the ocean turns red, and in spite of all the pounding and the hollering, they all come in and . . . rip you to pieces.

The monologue continues—as he details the days passing, the hundreds of men lost, the thousands of sharks converging, a body bitten in half and bobbing like a top, their eventual rescue. Call up the speech on YouTube, or, better yet, make a bowl of popcorn and screen the film for the full effect. It's more than Robert Shaw's slurred, deep-throated delivery; it's more than the brute power of the story; it's more than the lap of the water and the creak of the ship giving way to sinister violins that makes this scene work. It's the timing; it's the placement alongside a moment of laughter and face-splitting grins. We're vulnerable to the terror because we don't see it coming. Steven Spielberg understands the art of the reversal. He gives his audience a tickle and then slugs them in the stomach.

That's why every sex scene in a horror film gives way to a pitchfork to the abdomen, a head lopped off by a machete—because our arousal makes us more vulnerable, the scare more unexpected. And that's why this line works so well: "My mother believed that if you go out of your way to be friendly to people, they will take a liking to you, but this philosophy did not work for me, because I was a leper." This is the first sentence of "Buddy the Leper," a short story by Garrison Keillor. He lulls you with the opening platitude, and then surprises you with *leper,* a word that is the equivalent of a trapdoor into a ball pit.

I recently attended a performance of Sean O'Casey's *Juno and the Paycock* at the Guthrie Theater in Minneapolis. Normally I research plays beforehand, but I had been on the road, so I walked in blind, knowing absolutely nothing apart from the title. I soon learned that it takes place in Dublin during the Irish Civil War of the 1920s. A family of four is crammed into a tenement apartment with crumbling, water-stained walls and furniture held together with wire. Though they are desperately poor, not knowing how they'll afford their next meal, the father—known as "Captain" Jack because of his history as a merchant sailor—boozes away what little money they have at the corner pub. I laughed my way through so much of the first act, as Jack bickers with his wife and jokes with his pal and complains about "the pain in me legs, the pain in me legs" when presented with a possible job offer that would take him away from his boozing and loafing. He is a lovable loser, a ne'er-do-well who hoots and dances when a solicitor informs him of a windfall inheritance that will seemingly save his family.

It doesn't. His wild spending habits—and a problem with his will—leave the family horribly in debt, ruined. The furniture they bought on credit is repossessed. The solicitor gets Jack's daughter pregnant and then leaves the country. His son is killed by the IRA. His wife abandons him. And we are left, at the end of the play, with a wonderfully haunting image: Jack, drunk, alone, passed out on the floor of his empty apartment. At the Guthrie, the dim spotlight lingered for what felt like a long minute of total silence. A silence that felt cavernous given how loudly we had laughed over the past three hours. At intermission, I could never have guessed how carved out the play would leave me.

This matches my experience at the AWP conference a few years ago, when I heard Eula Biss read from "Time and Distance Overcome." I was unfamiliar with the author and the essay—and I think this is one of the reasons it destroyed me so fully. I wasn't ready for what was coming, caught off-balance. She read in a monotone voice, lulling the audience: "The idea on which the telephone depended— the idea that every home in the country could be connected by a vast network of wires suspended from poles set an average of one hundred feet apart—seemed far more unlikely than the idea that the human voice could be transmitted through a wire." It was a history lesson, it seemed, about the advent of the telephone and the infrastructure it demanded and the resistance it faced. I tuned in with the same mild interest I might give to a special about narwhals on the Discovery Channel.

Ten minutes later, she paused. It was a long pause. And in the essay, on the page, you can put a finger on that pause, a visual break that serves as a fulcrum point. Everything tips; the essay darkens. "In 1898, in Lake Cormorant, Mississippi, a black man was hanged from a telephone pole. And in Weir City, Kansas. And in Brookhaven, Mississippi. And in Tulsa, Oklahoma, where the hanged man was riddled with bullets. In Danville, Illinois, a black man's throat was slit, and his dead body was strung up on a telephone pole. Two black men were hanged from a telephone pole in Lewisburg, Virginia. And two in Hempstead, Texas, where one man was dragged out of the courtroom by a mob, and another was dragged out of jail." The list of atrocities continues, flatly stated. An ordinary object, the telephone pole, is unexpectedly redefined, invested with extraordinary power.

By the end of her reading, the audience was flattened. I looked around, stunned and amazed, and saw so many people shaking their heads, roughing away tears. I can't imagine Biss having the same effect on her audience if the essay dove directly into darkness.

Ursula K. Le Guin uses the same strategy in her short story "The Ones Who Walk Away from Omelas." It opens with a lengthy description of an idyllic community. Omelas is "bright-towered" by the sea. Music plays in the streets—"a shimmering of gong and tambourine"—and people dance to it. In a "great water-meadow" naked boys and girls run alongside horses with "their manes . . . braided with streamers of silver, gold, and green." Everyone is happy. There are flowers, booze, orgies. The descriptions stack up until halfway through the story, a question is posed: "Do you believe?"

The answer is no. You don't believe. Not in the festival, the city, the nauseating joy. Not until Le Guin tells us one more thing about this seeming utopia:

> In a basement under one of the beautiful public buildings of Omelas, or perhaps in the cellar of one of its spacious private homes, there is a room. It has one locked door, and no window. A little light seeps in dustily between cracks in the boards, secondhand from a cobwebbed window somewhere across the cellar. In one corner of the little room a couple of mops, with stiff, clotted, foul-smelling heads, stand near a rusty bucket. The floor is dirt, a little damp to the touch, as cellar dirt usually is. The room is about three paces long and two wide: a mere broom closet or disused tool room. In the room a child is sitting. It could be a boy or a girl. It looks about six, but actually is nearly ten. It is feeble-minded. Perhaps it was born defective, or perhaps it has become imbecile through fear, malnutrition, and neglect. It picks its nose and occasionally fumbles vaguely with its toes or genitals, as it sits hunched in the corner farthest from the bucket and the two mops. It is afraid of the mops. It finds them horrible. It shuts its eyes, but it knows the mops are still standing there; and the door is locked; and nobody will come.

It is covered with sores because it sits in its own excrement. It used to scream at night, but now it only whines and mewls. Its ribs show and its belly protrudes from starvation. It cannot remember sunlight or its mother's face.

Now we believe. We believe in light because of shadow; we believe in good because of evil, the balance that is the balance of life. Your stories and scenes require something similar: constant reversals, a modulation of tone and content, sometimes gently and sometimes jarringly negotiated, so that we will believe and so that we will feel moved to laugh or gasp or sob.

Sounds Like Writing

Unless you're a slob, if you're going out—to an opera or a thrash metal concert, a hot dog stand or a Michelin-rated French restaurant, a fall rodeo or a summer baseball game or a subzero skiing completion—you vary your wardrobe, dress accordingly. Black tie, bow tie, no tie. Watch cap, ball cap, ten-gallon Stetson. Flip-flops, shit-kickers, Nunn Bush wing tips shined to an opal glow. The same should go for your sentences. It's time to start thinking more carefully about style.

Musicians know what I'm talking about. Add some Johnny Cash to your playlist, select a song like "Five Feet High and Rising." He starts off with a hard strum and a question of mild concern, "How high's the water, Mama?" The response: "Two feet high and rising." A flood has come and the muddy water is creeping over the wheat and oats, seeping into the beehives, chasing chickens into the willow trees, reaching past the knees of a panicked cow. Every time Cash asks the question "How high's the water, Mama?" the water burbles up—from two to three, four, five feet high—and so does the tempo hurry, adding a sense of panic. This is complemented by the rising pitch and rising volume, the guitar and Cash's voice notching up and up and up, as though aurally climbing onto furniture, the roof, heightening the anxiety. The style replicates the content.

In order to make a political statement, Jimi Hendrix—in his Woodstock performance of "The Star-Spangled Banner"—perverts the style of a song so many hold dear. When he first takes the stage, the electric guitar wails and trembles, but the song still feels familiar, recognizable, as he eases us into the anthem. Minutes later, the dissonance takes over. Instead of bringing our hands to our hearts, we want to slam our hands over our ears, muffle a sound like saw blades cutting through bone, rakes dragging across concrete. The style of the song expresses the 1969 revolutionary's cry that the American dream has become the American nightmare.

You can do the same on the page. James Baldwin plays his own kind of music in the short story "Sonny's Blues." In the final scene, the narrator observes his brother, Sonny, taking the stage in a jazz club:

> And Sonny hadn't been near a piano for over a year. And he wasn't on much better terms with his life, not the life that stretched before him now. He and the piano stammered, started one way, got scared, stopped; started another way, panicked, marked time, started again; then seemed to have found a direction, panicked again, got stuck. And the face I saw on Sonny I'd never seen before. Everything had been burned out of it, and, at the same time, things usually hidden were being burned in, by the fire and fury of the battle which was occurring in him up there.

Observe the halting rhythm—"stammered, started one way, got scared, stopped"—the design musical but clumsy, like Sonny's fingers fumbling the ivories. A comma is a quarter rest, a semicolon a half rest, a period a full rest. We're jerking along erratically, intentionally.

And then the sentences begin to open up as Sonny begins to find his sound, to lose himself in the music, to connect with the piano, the band. It is in this moment that the narrator—a buttoned-up math teacher, so separate from and uncomprehending of Sonny's life as a heroin addict and blues musician—seems to finally understand his brother. His voice, the voice of the story, bends around the music, like a secret shared between siblings:

> Something began to happen. And Creole let out the reins. The dry, low, black man said something awful on the drums, Creole answered, and the drums talked back. Then the horn insisted, sweet and high, slightly detached perhaps, and Creole listened, commenting now and then, dry, and driving, beautiful and calm and old. Then they all came together again, and Sonny was part of the family again. I could tell this from his face. He seemed to have found, right there beneath his fingers, a damn brand-new piano. It seemed that he couldn't get over it. Then, for awhile, just being happy with Sonny, they seemed to be agreeing with him that brand-new pianos certainly were a gas.
>
> Then Creole stepped forward to remind them that what they were playing was the blues. He hit something in all of them, he hit something in me, myself, and the music tightened and deepened, apprehension began to beat the air. Creole began to tell us what the blues were all about. They were not about anything very new. He and his boys up there were keeping it new, at the risk of ruin, destruction, madness, and death, in order to find new ways to make us listen. For, while the tale of how we suffer, and how we are delighted, and how we may triumph is never new, it must always be heard. There isn't any other tale to tell, it's the only light we've got in all this darkness.

The sentences are full of slant rhymes, repetitions. Appositive phrases pile up in layers, like instruments that shout and fade over the top of one another. There are tiny lists, like a cluster of quickly fingered notes. And there are big sentences next to small sentences, like someone pulling on a trombone while someone else shakes a tambourine. Punctuation gets slippery, as in the last line of the story, where a comma takes the place of a period, like a stuttery blast of a brass horn.

Baldwin is one of the great prose stylists. So is Annie Dillard, who also plays around with sound in her memoir, *An American Childhood*. When talking about her father, she writes:

> New Orleans was the source of the music he loved: Dixieland jazz, O Dixieland. In New Orleans men would blow it in the air and beat it underfoot, the music that hustled and snapped, the music whose zip matched his when he was a man-about-town at home in Pittsburgh, working for the family firm; the music he tapped his foot to when he was a man-about-town in New York for a few years after college working for the family firm by day and by night hanging out at Jimmy Ryan's on Fifty-second Street with Zutty Singleton, the black drummer who befriended him, and the rest of the house band. A certain kind of Dixieland suited him best. They played it at Jimmy Ryan's, and Pee Wee Russell and Eddie Condon played it too—New Orleans Dixieland chilled a bit by its journey up the river, and smoothed by its sojourns in Chicago and New York.

The lyricism of this paragraph makes me want to stomp my feet and clap my hands. The first line is like a pronouncement: her father's love of jazz will intoxicate these sentences, and sure enough, they're dazzled with bluesy riffs, punctuated by repetition and that half-beat semicolon, and the words themselves convey a sound: *blow, beat, hustled, snapped, zip, tapped, chilled, smoothed*. Every sentence in her memoir sings. Like Nabokov, Dillard is rarely subdued, more often writing at top volume and with gymnastic flexibility. Here's another passage to consider, this one capturing a moment when she engages in one of my favorite childhood pastimes: chucking snowballs at traffic. On this occasion, a car stops. And a man gets out. And pursues them:

> He chased Mikey and me around the yellow house and up a backyard path we knew by heart: under a low tree, up a bank, through a hedge, down some snowy steps, and across the grocery store's delivery driveway. We smashed through a gap in another hedge, entered a scruffy backyard and ran around its back porch and tight between houses to Edgerton Avenue; we ran across Edgerton to an alley and up our own sliding woodpile to the Halls' front yard; he kept coming. We ran up Lloyd Street and wound through mazy backyards toward the steep hilltop at Willard and Lang.
>
> He chased us silently, block after block. He chased us silently over picket fences, through thorny hedges, between houses, around garbage cans, and across streets.

She uses a semicolon because she doesn't want a full rest, her punctuation as much of a sound directive as sheet music. The serial use of *and*—a nifty rhetorical trick called polysyndeton—adds to this effect. So do *around, up, under, through, down, across, between:* a string of prepositions that leaves the reader good and breathless, as we if we were the ones pounding through the neighborhood. And in this way the momentum is enhanced.

We feel a comparable sense of panic when watching a Paul Greengrass film. The director—of *United 93, Bloody Sunday, The Bourne Ultimatum, The Bourne Supremacy, Captain Phillips*—is known for his use of handheld cameras. The "shaky cam" effect provokes a sense of realism beyond documentary. As a viewer, you feel that you are a character, jolted by a bomb, splattered by water, thunking up and down stairs. There is a claustrophobia that sets in, a frazzled nervousness that suits his high-octane material (hijackings, bombings, superspies on the run). If he were guest-directing an episode of

Downton Abbey, of course, this style would be completely unsuitable, unless the servants—led by an Uzi-toting Mrs. Hughes—decided to rise up and take control of the estate by force.

Dillard makes us breathless—Greengrass makes us panicked and nauseated—and a similar stylistic decision gives *flow* to the opening of "The Hunter's Wife," a short story by Anthony Doerr. The hunter, on his first trip out of Montana, awakens on the plane "stricken still with the hours-old vision of ascending through rose-lit cumulus, of houses and barns like specks deep in the snowed-in valleys, all the scrolling country below looking December—brown and black hills streaked with snow, flashes of iced-over lakes, the long braids of a river gleaming at the bottom of a canyon." Maybe there is no better word than Doerr's own *scrolling* to capture the sensation of staring out a porthole window—the sentence, like the landscape, unfurls.

Now, if we took this same passage but put the character on a train instead of a plane, the delivery might be remarkably different—the sentences might be short and hard-hitting, made to match the *chu-chunk, chu-chunk* rhythm of a barreling train. Out a plane's window, everything slides along gradually, whereas when riding on Amtrak, you might catch only a glimpse of a farmhouse, an old oak tree, a truck waiting at a crossing. So maybe the sentences would work better as fragments, a series of frozen images flashing past.

In *Telegraph Avenue*, Michael Chabon employs a technique similar to Doerr's scrolling. There is a sentence midway through the book that stretches over twelve pages. It is a dazzling feat of language, a blurred-fingered riff that no doubt made his computer smoke and crack in two like a Gibson guitar picked too long, too hard. At first glance, maybe it seems like a perfect example of style replicating content, as we follow a parrot orbiting houses, skittering to a stop on branches and windowsills, visiting all the novel's characters, who—like the East Bay avenue in Northern California where the story is set—find themselves in a state of rough transition. But there is such a thing as too much of a good thing.

Chabon writes big. His sentences lavishly uncoil. His hulking plots defy summary. When I read one of his novels, I feel a little like I do when I turn a corner at the San Francisco Museum of Modern Art and see the gorgeous sprawl and splatter of Jackson Pollock's *Lucifer*—when I crank up the volume on *Sgt. Pepper's Lonely Hearts Club Band*—awed, hypnotized, overwhelmed. What a stylist he is, powering out sentences that are the equivalent of executing a triple backflip on a bucking bull while juggling machetes and yodeling. And though I often feel ready to burst into applause when I finally reach a period, when I was reading *Telegraph Avenue,* the pyrotechnics began to tire my eyes, fray my nerves.

This didn't happen when I read Chabon's novel *The Amazing Adventures of Kavalier and Clay*—and it didn't happen when I read his murder mystery–speculative history mash-up, *The Yiddish Policemen's Union*—but the subject matter of *Telegraph Avenue* is more of a throwback to early Chabon. His maximalist style suits his maximalist stories, like the *zap!* and *pow!* sound effects of a comic book panel, but *Telegraph Avenue* aligns itself more with *The Wonder Boys*—and I have to say that I long for that book's more subdued lyricism, for quiet passages like this one, when Grady and his father-in-law "leaned on each other for a moment, crippled in [their] various extremities, looking out at the empty longues on the dock, at the sun hanging low over the bare yellow hills." Compare this to the crank-it-up technique of *Telegraph Avenue:* "Steeled by a lifetime of training in the arts of repression, like Spock battling the septenary mating madness of the *pon farr,* Gwen had resisted the urges and surges of estrogen and progesterone for each of the first thirty-four weeks of her pregnancy, denying all cravings, battened down tight against hormonal gusts."

The twelve-page sentence begins:

If sorrow is the consequence of pattern spoiled, then the bird
was grieving, seeking comfort in the patter and tap of the
baby's shoes against the wooden floor, Rolando whaling away
like Billy Cobham with the heels of his little Air Jordans,
working himself around the room on his back, a human dust
mop making a knight's tour of the emptied-out living room,
brown eyes grooving with vacant fixity all the while on the
red tail feather and black eyebead of the parrot, for whose
care, removal, or ultimate disposition no instructions had
been given to Rolando's mother when she was directed to clear
out the place by the executor of the Cochise Jones estate, a
modest affair carefully depleted by sixty-plus years of foolish-
ness, most of what remained of it tied up in vinyl records, the
rest in vintage leisure suits (Aisha had counted twenty-two),
the fatal Hammond, a Yamaha keyboard on a cross-legged
metal stand . . .

On it goes until the parrot takes flight and the "scrolling" begins:

Luther saw against the afternoon sky the foreign profile of the
fugitive parrot making its escape, taking its bearings generally along the hypotenuse of Telegraph Avenue while parsing
light and scent and angles for their information, reckoning a
course toward the eucalyptus hills, thrown eastward by a sensation of horror as it skirted the death cloud hovering above
the Smokehouse hamburger stand, the sudden detour sending
it over the street of forgotten toys, over the tan bungalow lost
in flowers, where Fifty-Eight went unobserved by either of the
house's present occupants . . .

And on it goes still, but in this excerpt you can perhaps see the
swoop of the bird justifying the swoop of the sentence. Or not.
Your ultimate goal, as a storyteller, should be to sweep the reader

away. Pretty sentences exist only in the service of this goal. They are the incantations that enable the reader to dream with their eyes open, to believe in other worlds, to care about ink and paper as if they were flesh and blood. If you show off, if your prose is purple, if your writing "sounds like writing," then your reader will be aware they are reading a story, and when they are aware they are reading a story, the dream dissolves. Instead of letting the language invisibly enchant us, Chabon announces himself as sorcerer. The sentences put a spotlight on him and not the material.

A comic book reader is especially wowed by Superman's spandex-clad muscles, his ability to punch through steel and outrace a bullet, because his demeanor as Clark Kent is as buttoned-down as the collared shirt he wears to work at the *Daily Planet*. I would feel the same way about Chabon's twelve-page sentence if he evened out the stylistic spikes with a few more passages like the novel's lovely opener: "A white boy rode flatfoot on a skateboard, towed along, hand to shoulder, by a black boy pedaling a brakeless fixed-gear bike. Dark August morning, deep in the Flatlands. Hiss of tires. Granular unraveling of skateboard wheels against asphalt. Summertime Berkeley giving off her old-lady smell, nine different styles of jasmine and a squirt of he-cat." Hell yeah. More of this, please.

Doerr has a better sense of control. He knows we'll grow tired of his special effects. So he balances out fanciness with sparseness, and he modulates rhythm, expanding and contracting language, as though the page were breathing. And he'll follow a restricted sentence like this—"Now it was dark."—with something visually and sonically generous: "The airplane descended over Chicago, its galaxy of electric lights, the vast neighborhoods coming clearer as the plane glided toward the airport—streetlights, headlights, stacks of buildings, ice rinks, a truck turning at a stoplight, scraps of snow atop a warehouse and winking antennae on faraway hills, finally the long converging parallels of blue runway lights, and they were down."

He accomplishes in a few lines—a shotgun burst of lyricism—

what Chabon exhausts us with over twelve long pages. The plane sinks from the sky, and as the ground approaches, the images hit us faster now than when the plane ascended; the sentence is more clipped, hurried, almost panicked, matching the hunter's emotion (he's never been out of Montana before, after all, and he's here to see his estranged wife). And though of course the plane keeps rolling down the runway after the wheels screech on the asphalt, Doerr chooses to close the passage here—"and they were down"—because of the thudding finality of the action, with its simplicity (after so much poeticism) and impactful placement. I'm talking about the hunter's feelings, not just the act of ascending or descending in an airplane—the emotional circumstances, not just the physical—and this is to underscore how stylistic choices connect to the mood of the moment.

With this in mind, if you're writing about sex, maybe your aim is to arouse, in which case you probably want to use slippery, sensual language so that your sentences sound the way Marvin Gaye sings, smooth like "the silk that silk wears," to borrow a line from Adrian Matejka's poem "Understanding Al Green." But sex can be comical and awkward, too, and maybe that's what you're going for, if your character is a spectacled, acne-pocked, needle-necked teenage virgin more familiar with microscopes and textbooks than a woman's body, in which case the sentences might be halting and dotted with words like *unit* and *fornicate*.

Donna Tartt—in her novel *The Goldfinch*—maintains a thoughtful, controlled, even fussy past-tense point of view, but in the following scene she wants the reader to feel as the narrator does: drug-addled, alcohol-fogged. So her style, which has been robust but traditional so far, breaks down, the punctuation minimal, the sentences manic and jittery:

> Why did people get so worked up about it? I put on every piece of clothing in my suitcase (two shirts, sweater, extra trousers,

two pairs of socks) and sat sipping coca-cola from the mini-
bar and—still high and coming down—fell in and out of vivid
waking dreams: uncut diamonds, glittering black insects, one
particularly vivid dream of Andy, sopping wet, tennis shoes
squelching, trailing water into the room behind him something not quite right about him something weird looking little
bit off what's up Theo?

not much, you?

not much hey I hear you and Kits were getting married
Daddy told me

cool

yeah cool, we can't come though, Daddy's got an event at
the yacht club

hey that's too bad

and then we were going somewhere together Andy and
me with heavy suitcases we were going by boat, on the canal,
only Andy was like no way am I getting in that boat and I was
like sure I understand, so I took apart the sailboat screw by
screw, and put the pieces in my suitcase, we were carrying it
overland, sails and all, this was the plan, all you had to do was
follow the canals and they'd take you right where you wanted
to go or maybe just right back where you started but it was a
bigger job than I'd thought, disassembling a sailboat, it was
different than taking apart a table or chair and the pieces were
too big to fit in the luggage and there was a huge propeller
I was trying to jam in with my clothes and Andy was bored
and off to the side playing chess with someone I didn't like the
looks of and he said well if you can't plan it out ahead of time,
you'll just have to work it out it as you go along.

The drugs—and the narrator's bewildered, panicked state of mind—
infect the page. Capitalization absents itself. The voices of different
characters babble into each other, smear together. The sentences run

on breathlessly, stylistically hopped-up, strung-out, so that your eyes bug and your heart hurries.

And you should consider this your charge. Your own character might not be high, but they might be grieving or they might be terrified or they might be shy or they might be horny. Your own character might not be in a plane or a jazz club, but they might be in an avalanche or a car chase or a gunfight or an underground sex club. Wherever they are, however they are, should tone the sentences, replicate the experience in a complementary correspondence that will make your reader feel as they do.

Move Mountains
Activating Setting

I.

People are always asking why I write about Oregon, a question I find bewildering. That's where I grew up, after all. That's the place I've lived longer than anywhere else. And on so many levels it's a dynamic, fractured environment, a great stage for drama. The Cascade Mountains fence the state in half—the east side is high desert, the west side rain forest and pasture that runs into ocean. It's politically divided as well, the spur-jangling rural areas at odds with the hempy vortexes of liberalism you'll find in Portland and Eugene. And it's culturally confused, with the influx of Hispanics and rich, retired Californians. I could go on—about meth sheds and snowmobiles, vultures wheeling in the sky and rattlesnakes coiling under porches—but I'll save it for the fiction. Why do I write about Oregon? Why wouldn't I write about Oregon?

Place matters. That's what so many people seem to have forgotten. Is it because they spend most of their time indoors or online—so that they've lost touch with their environment? Is it because every city contains the same neon-and-concrete gauntlet of Targets, Little Caesars, Subways, Great Clips—so that every place looks like every other place?

Someone once told me, "I want my work to feel like it could happen anywhere."

To which I responded, "Huh." That's like saying you want your character to seem like she could be anyone, Margaret Thatcher or Pippi Longstocking, or you want your story to seem like it could happen anytime, a thousand years ago or a thousand years in the future. Abstraction sucks. Good writing relies on the particulars.

Maybe your character wears a pale blue bathrobe all day, every day, stitched with extra pockets that jangle with cigarette lighters and screws and marbles. Maybe your story takes place in the era when the Beach Boys blasted from radios and cars sported white-wall tires and boys slicked back their hair and rolled cigarette packs in the sleeves of their white T-shirts. This same standard applies to place.

Brady Udall—my former professor and the author of *The Lonely Polygamist*—once warned me that 75 percent of fan mail sneaks in a critical remark about how there isn't a meatpacking plant in this town or a green fire hydrant on that street or an old oak tree at the intersection of Empire and Seventh. And he was right. That's one of the reasons I don't often write about Illinois or Wisconsin or Iowa or Minnesota or any of the other places I've briefly lived in my nomadic adulthood. I don't know them well enough.

It takes a long time to know a place. I'm not talking just about its geography. I mean its history, its culture, its politics, its myths. Does Bigfoot or the hodag lurk in its woods? Is Elvis Presley or Paul Bunyan its most famous citizen? Can you see the northern lights coloring the horizon? Did the river, once so full of chemical runoff, catch fire and burn for three days? Is there a hot air balloon festival every August? How do they pronounce the word *roof* or *bagel*? Know a place the way Cheryl Strayed knows the Pacific Crest Trail, the way García Márquez knew Macondo and Hawthorne knew New England and Faulkner knew Yoknapatawpha County.

When I ask people to tell me something interesting about where they live, they often say, "Nothing." Maybe if you're from a place that isn't a booming metropolis or a tourist destination you think it's an unworthy stage for fiction. Look closer. Start listing off curiosities. Let's say you're in a small town in Iowa. How about the way, when the wind shifts just so, the air smells like the slaughterhouse twenty miles north? How about the murder-suicide that happened five years ago in the house across from the high school? How about the radioactive waste buried beneath the soccer fields? How about the tornadoes that unspool from the sky every spring and vacuum up the earth? How about last summer's flood, the one so bad that people were canoeing down Main Street? How about the clouds stacked up like mountains and the fertilizer that runs off the corn-fields and mucks up the rivers? How about the bluegrass band that made it big and tours internationally but still lives on a hobby farm outside town?

Write about your own backyard. Claim your own forty acres. Create a stage on which your characters will perform.

When a reader first picks up a story, they are like a coma patient—fluttering open their eyes in an unfamiliar world, wondering, *where am I, when am I, who am I?* The writer has an obligation to quickly and efficiently place the reader in the story.

Which is why writers should avoid opening with dialogue. I know, I know—you can think of ten thousand awesome stories that do exactly that. I still think it's a mistake. With one exception— "Where's Papa going with that ax?"—from the beginning of *Charlotte's Web*. It works because E. B. White fills the white space, immediately establishing three characters, one of them in the middle of an arresting gesture.

And that is your job: to fill in the white space. Imagine a blank canvas. Now imagine a sun *boing*ing up until it settles on an afternoon angle. Then a hundred or so trees spike themselves into a distant forest. A field of corn unfurls from the furrows—and a combine grumbles through it. In the cab of the combine sits a teenage boy with an Adam's apple the size of his fist. He's wearing Carhartt coveralls and has a cell phone pressed to his ear. His attention obviously isn't on the field—the combine is veering right—and from the gravelly roar below him, he ought to be powering down the engine: too much corn is getting mowed down too quickly. "You're sure?" the boy says, his voice pitched high. "You're sure you're ready?"

Maybe the boy is talking to his girlfriend and maybe she is at last ready to have sex with him at the gravel pit—or maybe he is talking to his father, who has decided to put the farm up for sale after a real estate developer expressed interest in building a subdivision on their land—or whatever. I'll trust that the mystery will drag my reader forward. Because at this point they are invested in a world and a character.

But what if I had opened with that line of dialogue? "You're sure? You're sure you're ready?" Not only would it mean nothing but it would be ungrounded, a genderless, ageless voice echoing through white space—and I would have to store it in my short-term memory and carry it with me for several sentences until it was at last contextualized. You don't want your reader working that hard at the start of a story. Moving from this world, with its myriad distractions, to the world of the page is hard enough. Place solidifies the otherworld we're entering and anchors your characters in it.

II.

Never give us a generic description. When we enter a new space, show it to us—but through a particular lens: your character's point of view, modified by mood.

So maybe we knob open the front door, step onto the porch, and . . . "The sky was a dying violet and the houses stood out darkly against it, bulbous liver-colored monstrosities of a uniform ugliness though no two were alike. Since this had been a fashionable neighborhood forty years ago, his mother persisted in thinking they did well to have an apartment in it. Each house had a narrow collar of dirt around it in which sat, usually, a grubby child."

In this passage—from Flannery O'Connor's "Everything That Rises Must Converge"—the setting is polluted by Julian's vision. He's a nasty piece of work. Bitter, jealous, insecure, spiteful. Most characters, when the sun sets, wax romantic about the halo of light burning behind a mountain or the pink and purple rafters lancing the sky. But to him the sky is "dying" and so is the neighborhood. The houses are ugly and dirty and "liver-colored." The grubby children don't play in the yards; they sit, as if stunned by their rotten surroundings.

He resents his childhood home, the place his mother was proud to raise him. This not only characterizes him but also contributes to narrative conflict. His mother wears dressy gloves, brags about her expensive hat, talks about how Julian's grandfather was a "prosperous landowner" and how his great-great-grandfather was a governor. She insists on their class—that they are a certain "kind of people"—a notion wrapped up in her very different perception of their surroundings. Julian is at odds with his environment, he is at odds with his mother, and we know something will snap as a result of this tension.

O'Connor is so good at this sort of thing that I can't help but include another example, this one from "The Artificial Nigger":

> Mr. Head awakened to discover that the room was full of moonlight. He sat up and stared at the floor boards—the color of silver—and then at the ticking on his pillow, which might have been brocade, and after a second, he saw half of the moon five feet away in his shaving mirror, paused as if it were waiting for his permission to enter. It rolled forward and cast a dignifying light on everything. The straight chair against the wall looked stiff and attentive as if it were awaiting an order and Mr. Head's trousers, hanging to the back of it, had an almost noble air, like the garment some great man had just flung to his servant.

Mr. Head lives up to his name. From this description he's obviously big*head*ed and thinks the world of himself. His vision makes silver out of wood. He imagines brocade rising lushly from his pillow.

The moon waits for his permission to enter. A chair is like a servant carrying the clothing of a great man. There's a hint in that paragraph that all is not as it seems: his shaving mirror is only five feet away. We might mistake him for royalty if not for a detail that implies cramped quarters. Soon we'll discover that his alarm clock is broken and sits on an overturned bucket. This inflated sense of self—demonstrated by the setting—will later bring trouble to the story.

David Fincher's adaptation of *Fight Club* does something similar. The Edward Norton character moves through his apartment and sees everything as it appears in a catalog: the price, the serial number, the product description. A coffee table in the shape of a ying-yang symbol, the Hovetrekke home exer-bike, all the IKEA products he believes define him as a person. Everything is factory-made, owned by tens of thousands of others. Nothing is unique; nothing has a story. His apartment has no soul. When he opens his fridge he fittingly finds it empty of everything except for condiments. His whole life is surface, no substance. His transformation as a character will be matched by his setting as he blows up his apartment and moves into the piss-stinking, rotten-walled animal den that is the house on Paper Street, the place where he will become truly wild and alive, a thing that bleeds and hungers. Through setting we get a stabilizing stage, a glimpse of his character, and a map of his emotional arc.

III.

Just as you should orient us in the beginning of a story, you should orient us throughout. Every time we jump to a new setting (whether that's a character boarding a plane or entering a locker room or dropping through an open manhole), we need to feel immediately stabilized.

Give us the New Mexico desert—give us the mining camp—give us the splintery whorehouse—give us the bedroom with peeling wallpaper and lace curtains—give us the brass bed on which your characters lie tangled. Not always in that telescoping order, but moving between the faraway and the nearby gives a sense of life, of three-dimensionality, the constant negotiation between place and space.

But simple staging isn't enough. A descriptive string like "There was a table. There was a lamp. There was a couch. There was a painting of hogs eating snakes" orients us, sure, but it's a passive construction. Make it active. Make it come alive.

A good portion of my novel *The Dead Lands* takes place in post-apocalyptic St. Louis. An expedition will later set off across the irradiated landscape in search of life, but before the quest begins, I needed to give my reader not only a sense of the Sanctuary—as the city is known—but also how the world has moved on. In an early draft, I delivered the geography and sociology like a kind of Wikipedia entry. It was mildly interesting but lacked oomph, movement, propulsion. So I added a robotic owl.

One of my central characters, Lewis, is a scholar, an inventor, a kind of magician. This owl—a hat-tip to one of the favorite films of my childhood, 1981's *Clash of the Titans*—is one of Lewis's devices. Its eyes can record and project and it serves as his spy:

The bird perches on the wall. It observes the prisoner hauled away, the crowd scattering, and then, with a creaking snap of its wings, it takes flight. It appears to be an owl, though not like any other in the world, made of metal and only a little larger than a man's fist.

Torches flare up all around the Sanctuary to fight the intruding night, and the owl's bronze feathers catch the light brightly when it flies from the wall, then over the gardens, the stables, the ropes of smoke that rise from chimneys and forges and ovens, the twisting streets busy with carts and dogs and bodies that stumble out of doorways. The wind blows cinders and dried bits of grass up into dust devils, and the owl blasts through them.

The skyscrapers and high-rises needle upward from the

center of the Sanctuary—Old Town, they call it—and the
mechanical owl darts between the canyons of them now. Some
of them still have windows, but most are open-air, so that they
appear like a vast and rotting honeycomb inside which people
crouch like brown grubs.

The owl's wings whirr. Gears snap and tick beneath its
breast. Within its glass eyes, an aperture contracts or expands
depending on whether the owl casts its gaze at light or
shadow.

This continues for another page and a half as the owl bombs
through the city and the point of view whirls around as we observe
the citizens that it startles in its passing—a blacksmith cooling a red
hinge in a bucket of horse piss, a dentist ripping a rotten tooth from
a mouth, a granny lounging on a balcony—and so this new world is
not only illustrated but activated.

I should not compare this weird, ridiculous sequence to *The Great
Gatsby,* but I'm going to, not because my work belongs on the same
shelf with Fitzgerald's, but because he's pulling off the same trick
more elegantly and quietly in this passage:

We walked through a high hallway into a bright rosy-colored
space, fragilely bound into the house by French windows
at either end. The windows were ajar and gleaming white
against the fresh grass outside that seemed to grow a little way
into the house. A breeze blew through the room, blew curtains
in at one end and out the other like pale flags, twisting them
up toward the frosted wedding-cake of the ceiling, and then
rippled over the wine-colored rug, making a shadow on it as
wind does on the sea.

The only completely stationary object in the room was an
enormous couch on which two young women were buoyed
up as though upon an anchored balloon. They were both in

white, and their dresses were rippling and fluttering as if they had just been blown back after a short flight around the house. I must have stood still for a few moments listening to the whip and snap of curtains and the groan of a picture on the wall. Then there was a boom as Tom Buchanan shut the rear windows and the caught wind died out about the room, and the curtains and the rugs and the two young women ballooned slowly to the floor.

Hot damn! I'm not the kind of guy who gets profanely exclamatory about descriptions of sitting rooms, but in this case I'll make an exception. Nothing is happening—outside of Nick walking into the room—and when nothing happens, stories stall. But in this case, Fitzgerald fights the lull by making everything come alive. The wind—his robot owl—does most of the work. Blowing and twisting curtains, rippling rugs and making pictures groan. Everything feels so animated, from the grass that "seemed to grow a little way into the house" to the windows that boom shut. The space is so physically active it might as well be a character.

I rarely see this, as obvious as the move may seem. More often space is treated as emotionally active. At its worst, the move comes across like so: the character looks out the window . . . and thinks about the pansies growing in the garden. The character stills, the landscape moves, some realization is achieved. The outer is a servant of the inner. Landscape as epiphany. La-di-da!

I get it. It works. I've done the same. I'm not asking you to stop doing this. I'm asking you to find other ways to activate the stage your actors occupy to make for a more engaging story. No one wants to watch a theater production of a man looking around his kitchen with his hands in his pockets, reciting a lengthy monologue about how he feels no regret for murdering his mother. Move those feet; unholster those hands. Rip open some drawers, withdraw some knives, chop some onions, make him knuckle away tears, even though he feels no grief, and try to splash the irritant away in the sink. Think about the visceral as much as the cerebral.

IV.

Setting should serve mood and theme. A wonderful example of this comes from *A River Runs through It*. Norman Maclean writes, "All things merge into one, and a river runs through it. The river was cut by the world's great flood and runs over rocks from the basement of time. . . . I am haunted by waters." From the very beginning to the very end, water and religion and family foam and roil together. But note that the characters aren't chilling in their Adirondack chairs. They spend a lot of time splashing through these waterways, hooking fish, fighting currents and each other.

This combination of the muscular and the mindful informs this excerpt from Cormac McCarthy's *All the Pretty Horses:*

> The horses stepped archly among the shadows that fell over the road, the bracken steamed. Bye and bye they passed a stand of roadside cholla against which small birds had been driven by the storm and there impaled. Gray nameless birds espaliered in attitudes of stillborn flight or hanging loosely in their feathers. Some of them were still alive and they twisted on their spines as the horses passed and raised their heads and cried out but the horsemen rode on. The sun rose up in the sky and the country took on new color, green fire in the acacia and paloverde and green in the roadside run-off grass and fire in the ocotillo. As if the rain were electric, had grounded circuits that the electric might be.

Setting is first something to overcome—to traverse and endure. It is miserably hot. We know that from the way the bracken steams and the sun hangs overhead and the acacia is described as "green fire." Everything appears as a threat. A storm has come through and with its winds has hurled birds into cactuses that speared them. Something electrical seems to snap in the air and carry the risk of shock. But beyond this—the obstacles of the landscape—the setting is projective as well. It forecasts terribly what awaits the horses around the next bend, when some predatory men will approach the boy in this company as prey.

Something similar happens in *The Texas Chainsaw Massacre*. A young couple wanders up to a dark-windowed, paint-peeling farmhouse in the middle of nowhere. The camera holds back as they climb the porch, as if it were afraid to draw too close. The man knocks on the door and while waiting for a response his shoe nudges what turns out to be a black-rooted tooth. "I've got something for you," he says to the young woman and drops it into her hand. She's frightened and revolted and leaves him in a huff. He should get the hell out of there, but of course he doesn't. He knocks again—and this time the force of his fist batters the door open. The angle shifts. We're inside now, looking out at him. The darkness of the interior harshly contrasts with the sun-bleached day and makes us even more uncomfortable: this is a place where even at noon it feels like midnight. He hesitates at the threshold, calling out, "Hello?" and "Is anybody home?" When we shift back to his perspective, we can see a lit doorway down the hall. The wall is red and crowded with skull and antler mounts. A blood-colored museum of the dead. The setting has alerted us: bad things are going to happen in this place. There is a sound—what might be the squealing of a pig—that draws him inside. He hurries forward, stumbles over something on the floor, and here—before the red wall of skulls—Leatherface appears, striking him in the temple with a mallet, dragging him out of sight, and then slamming a metal door shut with a heart-stopping boom. This is one of the most frightening scenes in film, thanks in large part to the way the setting is managed. The stage anchors us and the staging engages us.

Sometimes I'll sketch out a scene quickly and then return to it

later to fill in the blanks. I might have something that's purely dialogue, like this:

"Hey."

"Hey yourself."

"We need to talk."

"Okay."

"I need to tell you something."

"Okay."

"I'm late."

"To what?"

"I'm late."

"Oh."

"So I took the test. And it's positive."

"You're positive? I mean, you're sure?"

"Yes."

"Wow."

I'll be thinking about gestures, of course—the way he knifes into
his steak, shrieks the blade across the plate, the way she crosses her
arms as though hugging herself—but I'm also going to play around
with staging. I'll build a set and make the characters interact mean-
ingfully with it.

Maybe the sun is low in the sky, so that its light streams through
the window. It could throw black bars of shadow across the couple,
contributing to a sense of sudden imprisonment. Or maybe I would
station one of them in front of the window—say, the woman—so
that he would have to squint to see her. If she moves to the window
on purpose, it contributes to her character (she wants to shield her
own wounded expression from him). If she wanders there absent-
mindedly, it could contribute to mood, making him feel visually as
well as emotionally bewildered. I might put it right after the line
"So I took the test. And it's positive." And maybe I'd interrupt his
follow-up with a gesture; after he says, "You're positive?" I'd have
him lift a hand to shade his eyes, adding another beat before he says,

"I mean, you're sure?" If the linoleum floor or Formica counter is peeling at the edges, it could contribute to the frayed emotions of the moment and it could also add to his character (he doesn't take care of his house, so he won't take care of a baby)—I might lead or close with that. Maybe there's a parrot in a cage, rattling the bars, cackling and whispering cuss words. This could give the moment a more menacing, chaotic feel. Or maybe the bird is almost infantile, something he adores but she despises, something that's always come between them. There are infinite possibilities. Tea kettles could whistle, phones could ring. The carpet could be stained, the radio could be playing, the kitchen could be in the middle of a remodel. Or what if it was a restaurant instead? Or a park? Or a rodeo, a Fourth of July parade, a hospital waiting room, a cleared-out college classroom after a bio exam?

At the art museum, I love a good still life, but on the page, I'm looking for a more animated landscape that will transport and engage me. Give us a lantern-lit cave and make us feel fear. Give us a suburban neighborhood and make us feel phonily manicured and trapped. Give us a snow-scalloped slope and then send your lost hikers across it. Give us a reservoir that goes deeper than any anchor and then send some divers into it to retrieve a body. Give us a neon-lit strip and then send your teenagers down it in one of their moms' station wagons. Setting can go from being one of the most lifeless to one of the most lively and functioning ingredients in your stories.

Feckless Pondering

A student submitted to workshop a story about a convenience store robbery. With a gun to his head, the clerk emptied the register and thought about life and death. If he was shot, he would never walk barefoot across Hawaii's white sand beaches, never finish his degree and become a veterinarian, never run a marathon or go deep-sea fishing. He wanted to hug his grandmother and eat her chocolate-chip cookies. He wanted to live.

The instructor was Barry Hannah, the legendary Southern writer. He asked the student to read aloud the stick-up passage. Then he reached into his satchel, pulled out a handgun, and shoved it in the student's face. "What are you thinking about right now?" he said.

This story isn't true—I've heard a dozen different versions of it, like so many other Barry Hannah stories—but I wish it were, and let's pretend for a moment it is, since it calls out so perfectly the momentum-killing proclivity of so many writers to mash together action sequences with emotional fuss.

What was the student thinking? Nothing. He wasn't thinking about anything, the world crushed down to the black bore of the muzzle. He might have felt the urine sheeting his thigh and he might have heard the whimper escaping his mouth, but otherwise his thoughts were lost in a white-hot tangle. Later, after the gun was holstered, after the danger passed, *then* he could have wept with relief and sniffed a flower and eaten Grandma's chocolate-chip cookies with a renewed appreciation for life. But not in the moment. Let the action speak for itself.

Here is another workshop story, this one true, though not nearly so interesting. When I was in grad school, a fellow student handed in a story that contained the phrase *fecklessly pondered*. Grad students are two-faced creatures, sometimes friendly and supportive, but more often jealous and spiteful, and this was one of those cruel moments when they behaved like fifteen starved dogs attacking the same pork chop: they spent at least fifteen minutes talking about the godawfulness of *fecklessly pondered*, surely the most ridiculous pairing of words in the history of literature. *Feckless pondering* became a kind of tagline for our cohort. We would scribble it in the margins of stories, bring it up in workshop whenever someone turned our gaze away from the action and toward the navel.

There is nothing wrong with characters thinking, nothing wrong with repose, so long as it is strategically employed. Literary writers tend to overdo thoughtfulness, to glut their fiction with interiority that interferes with the reader getting swept away, just as many genre writers tend to neglect interiority in favor of action. One is bloated and precious, the other swift but without substance. On the one hand you have Jeffrey Eugenides's *The Marriage Plot*, and on the other, Dan Brown's *Inferno*.

A buddy of mine told me a story about training for the Coast Guard. In dive school, during Hell Week, he sat at the bottom of a pool and the instructor tore the air regulator from his mouth and knotted it around his manifold. He was supposed to stay cool, not panic, and try to hold his breath while unknotting the regulator and then crawl from one side of the pool to the other. He failed, and when he rose gasping to the surface, puking up water and complaining about cramps and the heavy chlorine burning his eyes, the instructor kicked him in the ribs and said, "Suffer in silence, asshole."

Sometimes I want to punch through the page and say the same

to characters who too often unburden their thoughts, in part because they come across as whiners, navel-gazers, assholes. But my ultimate complaint is purely mechanical: you are gumming up the gears of your story, constantly halting its progress. It's the equivalent of a buzzkill.

Envision your narrative topographically. The peaks—when a car crashes, a couple argues, a storm knocks out the power—should be balanced out by valleys, so that your story resembles Colorado instead of Iowa.

Traditionally, one of the sharpest peaks comes at the beginning. You want to grab your reader by the throat and drag them down the rabbit hole. In a thriller, like Richard Lange's *Angel Baby,* the wife of a drug lord attempts to escape his Tijuana compound. In a horror novel, as in Stephen King's *It,* the monster attacks when Pennywise the clown peeps his face out of the sewer, offers a balloon to a boy, and then rips off his arm as he reaches for it. In a fantasy novel, like George R. R. Martin's *Game of Thrones,* a mysterious presence haunts the woods north of the Wall and hunts down a group of rangers.

These openings spike our adrenaline, urge us on with page-turning hunger, but they also typically set up an antagonistic force, the central trouble of the narrative. Only afterward do we come to understand the implications of the attack or wreck or kidnapping. Follow the visceral with the cerebral.

Lauren Groff's short story "Delicate Edible Birds" opens up with an extraordinarily vivid and gripping set piece. A group of journalists huddles in a jeep, waiting for a photographer named Lucci. This is in 1940, after the surrender of Paris, and he has headed off to take photos of the Germans as they march into the city. At last he appears, pedaling madly on his bicycle, saying, "Gogogogogo." He is pursued by what appears to be the whole German army. Planes with swastikas on their wings roar overhead and soldiers on motorcycles zoom after them holding pistols.

They make their escape, and only then does Lucci tell them about the photo, the one that will make him famous, the one of the Nazis goose-stepping past the Arc de Triomphe. It is at this point that he discovers the bullet hole in his trousers and promptly vomits into a ditch. The journalists are in the country now, hidden away in a copse of hemlock, safe. A moment of calm during which we come to understand what they are doing in France and how they know Bern, the firebrand female reporter who will eventually both save them and ruin them. This pause, before they formulate a plan and move on again, gives the story both emotional currency and a chance to catch its breath.

In screenplays, around page 25, the first plot point occurs. Also known as a "doorway moment," this is when the main character makes a decision, in response to the inciting incident of the story, that is the beginning of their transformative arc. In *Star Wars,* after Stormtroopers burn down the moisture farm and kill his aunt and uncle, Luke Skywalker decides to escape Tatooine with Obi-Wan Kenobi and join the rebellion. In *Die Hard,* John McClane yanks the fire alarm, alerting the authorities that something fishy is going on and alerting the terrorists that someone else is in the building. In Tolkien's *The Fellowship of the Ring,* Frodo steps forward in Rivendell and says he will carry the ring to Mount Doom. In *The Matrix,* Neo decides to take the red pill and gives up the comfortable illusion of his previous life. These are called doorway moments because once the decision is made, a door closes behind the character: there is no going back.

There is no going back for Bern and her fellow journalists. After they escape Paris, they discover that the wires are cut in every city across France. The government is fleeing. There is nowhere to sleep. No food. No water. They make the decision to press on rather than flee, and in doing so they come across a farm, where they request food and shelter. Too late, they realize the farmer is a Nazi sympathizer with an eye for Bern.

These junctures need to be earned. The scenes that follow the inciting incident and precede the doorway moment often find the characters in repose, a necessary valley between two peaks. In Groff's "Delicate Edible Birds," the physical peril of the invasion and the romantic entanglements and the career aspirations of the group are established, so that later we understand how loaded and precarious the situation is when the farmer threatens to hand them over to the Nazis unless Bern sleeps with him. This is the equivalent of the scene in *Oceans Eleven* when the characters brainstorm how they might rob the Bellagio. The misfits gather in the living room and listen to George Clooney rattle off not only the amount of money in the vault but the dangers they will face—security cameras, laser-triggered alarms, guards with assault rifles, phone book–thick steel doors—before they all say, "I'm in."

These are the stakes of the situation. Without them, we won't care about the decision the character makes, the doorway they walk through. These scenes are essential and instructional, and they deserve their own space, apart from the melee surrounding them. Just as in life, we best process a long day on the wooded trail or dockside Adirondack, relaxation in the face of agitation.

As the story progresses, the action will heighten. There will be more shark attacks, more car chases, more gunfights and hauntings and nail-biting football games. Consider how much real estate they take up in your story, how many pages they account for, and then frame them with proportionate moments of repose. If you're stretching out the physical beats, then you need to stretch out the emotional beats as well. Going into the scene, what are the stakes of the situation? Following the scene, what are the implications of the action that just took place? Not only does this make the bang-'em-up, shoot-'em-up sequences resonate as more than pure spectacle, but it gives the narrative tonal and emotional variance.

Study George Orwell's classic essay "Shooting an Elephant" for evidence of this elegant balance of physical and emotional beats.

He opens with descriptions of betel juice spit on women's dresses at the bazaar, a Burmese tripping him on the football field, Buddhist priests jeering at Europeans from street corners—followed by a long, emotional paragraph that begins, "All this was perplexing and upsetting." This seesaw effect continues throughout. After a lengthy narrative sequence—during which he follows the trail of devastation left by the rampaging elephant and finally locates the animal in a paddy field—Orwell retreats inside his head and mulls over all the reasons he should not kill the elephant. It is "a huge and costly piece of machinery." Its "attack of 'must' was already passing off." And, the simplest reason of all, "I did not in the least want to shoot him." These feelings are complicated by the crowd of Burmese that surrounds him. They expect him to do it, and he can feel "their two thousand wills pressing me forward, irresistibly." He makes the decision to kill the elephant, and this doorway gives way to a painfully explicit passage about its sagging body and drooping head, the "long rattling gasps" of its breath as he fires bullet after bullet into it.

Physical, emotional, physical, emotional, back and forth. As William Kittredge is so fond of saying, "Tell a story, have some thoughts about it. Tell a story, have some thoughts about it."

You already know that the emotional and physical summit comes at the end of your story. The final fight. There is no juncture more critical. Whatever is won or lost—a trophy, a marriage, a job, a pile of gold, a reputation, a soul, a life—will matter to us only if you make it clear why it matters so much to your characters.

In literary fiction, this resolution is often referred to as the epiphany. Maybe no one handles it better than Frank O'Connor in his short story "Guests of the Nation." Two Englishmen are held hostage by the IRA during the War for Independence. There is a strong sense of camaraderie between the hostages and their captors, which makes the ending when the Englishmen must be executed all the more agonizing:

Then, by God, in the very doorway, she fell on her knees and began praying, and after looking at her for a minute or two Noble did the same by the fireplace. I pushed my way out past her and left them at it. I stood at the door, watching the stars and listening to the shrieking of the birds dying out over the bogs. It is so strange what you feel at times like that that you can't describe it. Noble says he saw everything ten times the size, as though there were nothing in the whole world but that little patch of bog with the two Englishmen stiffening into it, but with me it was as if the patch of bog where the Englishmen were was a million miles away, and even Noble and the old woman, mumbling behind me, and the birds and the bloody stars were all far away, and I was somehow very small and very lost and lonely like a child astray in the snow. And anything that happened to me afterwards, I never felt the same about again.

This is one of the most memorable denouements in all of literature. The trigger is pulled, the bullets are fired, the bodies fall, and our narrator's life spins out of control. He feels a "million miles away," separate from the farmhouse, separate from the stars, small, lost, miserable. He has followed through on his duty as a soldier and, in doing so, failed as a friend and blackly corrupted his soul. He'll never be the same. That's why the story matters.

"And anything that happened to me afterwards, I never felt the same about again" could conclude every story ever written. The Death Star has exploded—the Ring of Power has melted into Mount Doom's fiery chasm—Ivan Drago has been knocked flat—the shark has been killed—the Englishmen, at once friends and enemies, have been killed—but so what? The denouement is the answer, the emotional consequence of the physical warfare you have been building toward since the first line.

Make a graph of your story or novel or essay or memoir. Step back and judge it as a whole. Pay attention to how you might balance the physical beats and the emotional beats rather than entangle them. Tell a story; have some thoughts about it. Tell a story; have some thoughts about it. Then your feckless pondering will become feckful.

Get a Job

I married into a farm family. For four generations, in the northwest corner of Wisconsin, outside the wooded hamlet of Elk Mound—where the Packers rule and cheese is never far from the hand and the blasting white winters weaken you into something half-alive—my in-laws have risen at 4:30 every morning to milk their seventy-five Holsteins and to disc and plant and harvest their thousand acres of corn and soybeans.

Every few months, my wife and I make the two-hour trek from Minnesota to visit, the last time in the spring. After we heaved our suitcases inside and pulled up a chair at the kitchen table, my father-in-law came in from the barn, shook my hand, and said, "Corn up?"

He wanted to know where he stood compared to Minnesota farmers. He wanted to know whether the rain had let up, whether the tractors had grumbled through the fields, whether the first green shoots were springing from the furrows. I could say with certainty, "Yeah, corn's up, ankle-high," because I had looked. Because I knew he would ask. Just as I know he will ask in July, "Tasseled out yet?" and in September or October, "Harvesting?"

He's a dangerous driver; as we putter around Elk Mound, his attention flits so often from the road to the fields that we'll frequently find ourselves straddling the yellow line or skirting a ditch. With one hand on the wheel, he'll list off who owns what land, who needs a new combine, who's selling out to a developer ready to hammer together a subdivision. He'll brake along the shoulder to ogle a new manure spreader.

I admit to feeling puzzled when I first met him, when he asked me whether anyone in my family farmed, when every conversation somehow cycled back to chores or machinery or crop yield. It took me a few years to get used to his way of seeing the world. Now I anticipate it—and think of him every time I pass an implement dealer or gaze out over a rust-colored spread of soybeans after an autumn freeze.

And this is what so many beginning writers fail to realize—the same thing I failed to realize when I first met my in-laws: that your way of seeing the world bends around your work. We spend the majority of our adult lives hunched over a desk in a hive of cubicles, or fitting together auto parts in a factory assembly line, or scraping charred burger off a grill as a line cook, or stuck in traffic limbo somewhere between the boardroom table and the La-Z-Boy recliner. And yet in most of the student stories I read, work is mentioned only in passing or is absent altogether.

Whether we like it or not, work defines us. Work dominates our lives. And we have an obligation, in our prose and poetry, in the interest of realism, and in the service of point of view, voice, setting, metaphor, and story, to try to incorporate credibly and richly the working lives of our characters.

Point of view, as we well know, is the filter through which a reader observes a story. Any number of things will influence the perspective—whether a character was beaten or coddled by his parents—whether a character comes from Libya or Canada or Uzbekistan—whether a character can rack two hundred pounds on the bench or barely hoist a gallon of milk—whether a character has loved or grieved or betrayed or killed—whether a character lives in a time of war or a time of peace—whether a character is a rosy-cheeked seventeen or a gray-haired, glazed-eyed eighty—but chief among them is a character's job.

Let's say our character is an underwear model. Call him Samson.

Forget making him complicated and three-dimensional. For the moment, we'll happily wallow in stereotype. Samson walks into a room. Maybe he clacks his boot heels across the hardwood floor to make certain everyone turns to look when he first walks through the door. What does he see? Every reflective surface? A mirror, a window, a knife. Anything he might use to check his feathery hair, his bulging pecs. Or maybe he exploits the lighting, standing far from the chandelier that drags shadows across his face but close to a table lamp that gives off a soft glow. Maybe he inventories the designer labels—this man wears an Omega watch, that man a Rolex. Maybe he eyes the competition, determining who is taller, who is tanner.

The introduction to the Showtime series *Dexter* is similarly exaggerated. As the opening credits roll, the titular character (a serial killer played by Michael C. Hall) goes through his morning routine: a razor nicks his neck, an egg cracks like a skull, ketchup bloodily spots his plate, a tie nooses his neck. The possibility of violence is everywhere. Will Ferrell is no less a caricature in *Stranger than Fiction*. He plays Harold Crick, an IRS auditor of infinite calculations who is hardwired to notice numbers, to make formulations—calculating the number of steps it takes to get from his apartment to the bus, determining the most precise and efficient way to knot a tie, to load a dishwasher.

There are many versions of Harold Crick in Joshua Ferris's white-collar novel *Then We Came to the End*. The characters work in a Chicago advertising firm, and every day everyone wears some variation of the power suit or the long-sleeve button-down with ironed chinos. The characters are assigned to cubicles and glass-walled offices. They carry out the same actions over and over and over again, filling out spreadsheets, calculating earnings, sitting through endless PowerPoint presentations. And their story is told in the first-person plural:

> We were fractious and overpaid. Our mornings lacked promise. At least those of us who smoked had something to look

forward to at ten-fifteen. Most of us liked most everyone, a few
of us hated specific individuals, one or two people loved everyone and everything. Those who loved everyone were unani-
mously reviled. We loved free bagels in the morning. They
happened all too infrequently. Our benefits were astonishing
in comprehensiveness and quality of care. Sometimes we
questioned whether they were worth it. We thought moving to
India might be better, or going back to nursing school. Doing
something with the handicapped or working with our hands.
No one ever acted on these impulses, despite their daily, sometimes hourly contractions. Instead we met in conference rooms
to discuss the issues of the day.

This point of view might come across as gimmicky if not for
the circumstances: the work destroys individual identity, and the
employees become part of a capitalist collective, a conformist hive.
Boardroom rhetoric infects the voice: benefits "astonishing in comprehensiveness and quality of care," "printing errors, transposed
numbers," "call now and order today." This is what too many meet-
ings and instruction manuals and water-cooler conversations will
do to you.

Every now and then a character breaks away from the "we,"
and every now and then the sentences buck their slow, formal ca-
dence with a *fuck* or a *damn,* and every now and then the characters
yearn for something else, something brighter than the harsh glow
of the fluorescents overhead. But only for a moment. The voice is as
buttoned down as an Oxford pinstripe.

Compare this to the untrammeled voice and frayed-edge blue-
collar perspective of Kevin McIlvoy's "The People Who Own Pianos":

We never can find their fuckin houses.

We get a set of shit directions there, a different set of
shit directions back. Okay, we've got an attitude about the
goddamn load no matter what we're told it is—grand, baby,

standup, damaged, used, good used, or good—fifth or first floor, basement, attic, narrow or wide staircase—the kit or the whole coffin—it's the same to A.D. Moving.

We carry it out into the light beyond the lighted, decorated, dimwit room we rearrange, rip, gouge, and nick all we want on our way out. Make way, we say, make way—words that give us rights greater any day than the owners', am I right?

The piano mover encounters setting as a series of tight hallways, narrow staircases—and as an economic indicator. The world is broken down according to the haves and the have-nots. The people who own pianos are the people who have hot tubs, stainless-steel ovens, top-shelf scotch in the liquor cabinet, oxblood wingback leather chairs with gold buttons. Like Ferris, McIlvoy uses the first-person plural. However, in this case, the "we" is there to distinguish the "us" from the "them." The people who move pianos are not the people who own pianos. And like Ferris, McIlvoy supplies us with plenty of insider jargon—when he describes a grand versus a baby grand, "the kit or the whole coffin," "mummify[ing] the sound," "amputat[ing] the legs"—making us trust him and the credibility of the story.

But unlike Ferris, McIlvoy strips away all formality from the voice, the sentences punctuated and patterned to capture the rough-edged everyday chatter of somebody who might drag up a stool next to you at a bar. In the texture of the voice, I hear boots clomping up and down stairs, a heavy load gouging plaster—and there is music in this, like a country song writ large.

Sometimes I like to think of myself as a referee—dressed in my black-and-white stripes, whistle dangling from my neck—racing up and down the sides of student manuscripts. Every now and then, I will make a series of complicated hand gestures, screech my whistle, and say, "Point-of-view violation!" This is because the writer, after establishing a first-person or close-third point of view, has violated the constrictions of that perspective. In the first few sentences of a story, you establish a contract with your reader. You have violated that contract if you, say, leap from the gaze of a beachside sunbather to that of a pilot in a plane streaking by overhead.

Nor, tonally, should you build baroque sentences when the mind of your character is empty, his life unadorned. Her voice shouldn't sound like white lace and gold trim when her home reeks of cheap whiskey and wood smoke. The trucker should not have a laugh like a booming bassoon. The trucker should laugh like a hot tire ripping apart at eighty-five miles per hour. The kindergarten teacher should have Crayola-blue eyes, *not* gunmetal-blue eyes. Unless, of course, the title of the story is "Mrs. Snodgrass Finally Snaps." Point of view corrals description and metaphor—and the character's job determines the point of view.

Consider Brian Turner's poem "At Lowe's Home Improvement Center." The speaker, Turner, has served overseas and brought the war home with him:

> Standing in aisle 16, the hammer and anchor aisle,
> I bust a 50 pound box of double-headed nails
> open by accident, their oily bright shanks
> and diamond points like firing pins
> from M-4s and M-16s.

Turner hovers between two worlds, not at peace and not at war, not a marine and not a citizen, not a part of the United States and not a part of Iraq. A fan reminds him of the rotor wash of a Blackhawk, a cash register drawer has the rattle of chain gun, a dropped pallet booms like a mortar, paint pools in the aisles like blood. He cannot separate himself from his work. It is there, at every turn, imprisoning him.

A job also sets the story in motion.

It is a job in Walter Kirn's *Up in the Air* that leads Ryan Bingham to the woman who will make him crave something more substantial and authentic than his single-serving lifestyle. It is a job in Philip Levine's poem "You Can Have It" that yellows the hands and hunches the backs and shortens the breath and the lives of two brothers who work sliding ice blocks down chutes, stacking crates into boxcars. It is a job in Susan Orlean's *The Orchid Thief* that sends her into the swamps of Florida to a plant-poaching under-world in which she glimpses passion for the first time. It is a job in Margaret Atwood's *The Handmaid's Tale* that punishes Offred, a concubine, and makes her ultimately join a resistance faction that challenges the male dictatorship of her country.

It is a job that frames and sets into motion every element of your story or essay or poem—and it is *your* job to do the required research that will bring the language and tasks and schedule and perspective of your characters' work to life. Google can do only so much for you. The library can do only so much for you. You need to write from the trenches.

One way to approach this is to channel your past. The age-old writing maxim is, after all, to "Write what you know." That's what Mike Magnuson did in his novel *The Right Man for the Job,* drawing upon his time working as a repo man in Columbus, Ohio. That's what Pam Houston did in her memoir *A Rough Guide to the Heart,* about her experience as a river and hunting guide. The job doesn't have to be extreme—doesn't have to be romantic or dangerous or grotesque—to be compelling. You could do the same with your time making swirly cones at Dairy Queen or nannying for two snot-smeared little trolls or folding skinny jeans into perfect sharp-edged piles at American Eagle Outfitters.

So you could write what you know. The problem, of course, is that some people don't know shit. In which case, flip the rule on its head and know what you write. Tom Wolfe never walked on the moon, but that didn't stop him from writing *The Right Stuff,* a book he spent years researching, interviewing astronauts and visiting Cape Canaveral, making sure he secured every detail about the manned space program. I've never worked as a taxidermist, but I wrote a short story about one called "The Killing." I visited a taxidermy studio, stroked the polyurethane forms, clacked the glass eyeballs around in my palm, and sniffed the formaldehyde. I spent several days working with the employees, eavesdropping on their conversations, taking notes on the peculiar insider lingo I could never have gleaned from Wikipedia.

I used to dread research. Because I associated it primarily with the Panama Canal paper assigned to me by Mrs. Zeganhagen in my ninth-grade history class. Hours spent in the library, pulling books off the shelves, leafing through age-spotted pages, jotting down notes on three-by-five cards, fretting over MLA format.

On occasion, I still find myself deep in the stacks. Every story I write is a research project. If I'm writing about war, I read memoirs and novels on the subject, and I also watch documentaries, read blogs, dig up newspaper and magazine articles, print photos and artwork and advertisements—anything that might spur my imagination. I've heard that James Michener would read a hundred or more books on Alaska or Texas or Hawaii before he began to write his novels about those places, and though I'm not that obsessive, I immerse myself deeply in research and through it discover history and culture and geography and myth and language that will ultimately give my short story or novel authenticity.

But the research process has become so much more complicated and adventurous than going to the library. Consider this poem by David Lee, "Loading a Boar":

> We were loading a boar, a goddam mean big sonofabitch and
>   he jumped out of the
> pickup four times and tore out my stockracks and rooted me in
>   the stomach and I
> fell down and he bit John on the knee and he thought it was
>   broken and so did I

and the boar stood over in the far corner of the pen and watched
     us and John and I just sat there tired and Jan laughed and
     brought us a beer and I said, "John it aint
worth it, nothing's going right and I'm feeling half dead and
     haven't wrote a poem in ages
and I'm ready to quit it all," and John said, "shit, young feller,
     you aint got
started yet and the reason's cause you trying to do it outside
     yourself and aint
looking in and if you wanna by god write pomes you gotta
     write pomes about what you know and not about the rest
     and you can write about pigs and that boar
and Jan and you and me and the rest and there aint no way
     you're gonna quit," and
we drank beer and smoked, all three of us, and finally loaded
     that mean bastard
and drove home and unloaded him and he bit me again and I
     went in the house
and got out my paper and pencils and started writing and
     found out John he was right.

Call this method writing. You know all about method acting.
Christian Bale starved himself, losing more than sixty pounds for
his role in *The Machinist*. Dustin Hoffman famously remained awake
for two days to shoot the scene in *Marathon Man* when Sir Laurence
Olivier tortures him with a drill to the mouth. Alfred Hitchcock
hurled live seagulls at Tippi Hedren's face during the filming of
The Birds. In the same spirit, Hemingway hunted his way through
Africa and fished his way through northern Michigan. Sebastian
Junger embedded himself with a platoon of soldiers in Afghanistan.
Susan Orlean mucked through swamps with orchid hunters. I have
friends who have visited morgues and prisons and done ride-alongs
with cops for material. Maybe Virginia Woolf thought about going

to the lighthouse, but I doubt she ever got there, or the novel might have ended differently.

I have gone caving for material, climbed trees for material, gone driving off-road for material. I have gone to the gun range to fire an assault rifle and harvest sensory details: the hellish, sweet stink of gunfire, the kick of the recoil like a horse's hoof. I have leaped out of planes and climbed mountains and worn a pregnancy suit and drunk nothing but water and eaten nothing but fruits and vegetables for twenty-one days—all in the name of literature.

Red Moon was the most monstrous book I had ever written. I realized very quickly how little I knew about the subject matter. One of my characters is the governor of Oregon—and then a presidential candidate. Another works as a government agent. Another is a computer wizard—and still another a medical researcher who specializes in animal-borne pathogens.

I sat down with staff at the USDA, with faculty at Iowa State University. I bought them gallons of coffee and I scribbled my way through a stack of yellow legal tablets. From them I came to understand the slippery science of my subject matter. As I've written it, in seventh-century Scandinavia, as part of a winter solstice ceremony, people slaughter and eat a wolf to take in its power and cunning for the long, dark months ahead. A disease—similar to chronic wasting disease and mad cow disease—spreads from the wolf to the human population. Fast-forward to the present and 10 percent of the population is infected with a disease that is like an unleashed id, a wildness that cannot be contained except with medication. They have been victimized throughout history and nearly decimated during the Crusades, westward expansionism, World War II. They cannot hold certain jobs. They must take an emotionally deadening drug and succumb to monthly blood tests. They are part of a public registry. Of course there is an uprising, and that is where the novel begins.

From my interviews, I came to understand so much about how prions (not viruses, but a protein-based pathogen) inhabit and affect the body and mind, how to apply for grants, how to arrange a lab, how vaccines are developed and how politicized the process is. Altogether I might have spent forty hours on the phone with or across the table from experts who helped me better understand my own material.

I recently moved, and when digging through a box, I discovered an old research paper, written in the sixth grade. The title: "Werewolves!" In it are many pop references, some shoddy historical chronicling, a sampling of folklore, and then—in conclusion—a ceremony. The ceremony by which one will become a werewolf. I remember, so long ago now, on the night of the full moon, arranging a pentagram in my backyard and saying the words from a book I found in some dark corner of the library. When hair didn't bristle on my skin, fangs didn't grow from my gums, I walked back to my house, slump-shouldered, not knowing I was, in fact, infected.

Writing is an act of empathy. You are occupying and understanding a point of view that might be alien to your own—and work is often the keyhole through which you peer. Before I met my wife, before I heard my father-in-law's alarm blare at 4:30, before I saw him wax a tractor and peel a cowl off a birthed calf and shrug off an oil-stained set of coveralls and combine corn until midnight and toss straw bales into a barn loft and tear through pasture in a mud-splattered ATV, a barn was nothing but a red blur outside my car window. Now, after observing him and helping him work—the two of us scraping manure from the barn floor, picking up rocks in the fields—I understand the greater ways in which our work defines our character.

Get a job.

Consider the Orange
Meaningful Repetition

My son began to breathe raggedly in the night. A whistling rasp that worsened as his throat constricted. His coughing became a kind of barking. Croup, the doctor called it, an inflammation of the larynx and trachea. She strapped a mask to his face while I clutched him, held his struggling body for the hour-long nebulizer treatment, and while the oxygen tank hissed and the vapor made a cloud all around us, my son cried out in a hoarse voice that was not his own. An ambulance took him from the clinic to the ICU. His lips were turning blue. The fleshy bowl at the bottom of his neck depressed into shadow with every sucking breath. They shot him full of steroids. They pricked his arm with an IV. They ran an oxygen tube under his nose and he ripped it out. So they replaced the tube, this time taping it to his cheeks, and when he ripped it away again, he took the skin with it. There he was, in his diaper, in his tiny hospital gown with red and blue balloons on it, his tears mingling with the blood streaming down his cheeks, barely able to cry out in pain, his screams only worsening the inflammation.

For four days they kept him in the ICU. And during those four days we read Dr. Seuss books and put together farm animal puzzles—but for the most part he just wanted to watch movies. *Toy Story* was one of them—and *Toy Story* was the movie my son wanted to watch, over and over again. By the time we packed our bags and the doctors discharged us, we had watched it more than ten times. Years later, whenever I come across *Toy Story*—while flipping channels or walking through Target or Toys "R" Us—whenever I see Woody the cowboy flopping his body across the screen or hear Buzz Lightyear call out, "To infinity and beyond," I cringe and go dizzy as the old panic rises up in me again, the terrifying certainty that my son will stop breathing. A movie that makes most smile makes me snarl. It earned emotional currency through repetition, as it played over and over when I held my wheezing son, when the doctors traded out IV bags.

T. S. Eliot, in his 1920 volume *The Sacred Wood: Essays on Poetry and Criticism,* writes about the objective correlative—an external equivalent for an internal state of mind. Similar to imagism, the objective correlative demands the definite over the abstract, precision in place of generalization. So an object, a setting, an event, something crystallizes and doubles for mood, emotion. A symbol, in other words. You know all about this. How a cross represents faith, sacrifice, resurrection—so that the sight of a crucifix hanging from a neck or a character throwing out their arms or even a car driving through a crossroads elicits a certain emotion. How an American flag is a stand-in for freedom, patriotism, democracy—so that if we see one snapping in the wind or burning in the street or tacked upside-down to a wall, we feel consequently moved.

These, of course, are clichés—ready-made symbols with meaning already attached to them. To throw them into a story or an essay or a poem is to lazily roll your cart into the literary Walmart and pull them off the shelf like hundreds of thousands of poets and writers before you.

Consider my son's croup and realize that *Toy Story* continues to impact me—to surprise a frown out of me—in a way that walking into a hospital, despite the familiar fluorescent lighting and latex-and-ammonia smell, does not. Why? Hospitals are too easy, too familiar as a breeding ground for sadness and sentimentality. They're the place—at the end of, say, an episode of *Touched by an Angel*—where the pianos tremble and the light goes gauzy and a single tear races down a cheek. I see a hospital and my shields go up. Whereas *Toy Story*—even the Randy Newman sound track—sends me into the abyss.

Consider the orange. In each of Francis Ford Coppola's *Godfather* films, every time an orange appears, bad things happen. Sonny is gunned down after he passes a billboard for Florida oranges. Michael dies with an orange in his hand. Don Vito Corleone is ambushed by gunmen after shopping for oranges at an outdoor market—and later, after he's released from the hospital, after he returns to his estate, when picnicking with his grandson, he cuts into an orange and pops a slice into his mouth. He grins and bulges his eyes and pretends to be an ape. The boy runs and Vito gives chase—grunting, wheezing, finally collapsing, dead of a heart attack. Over and over again, the orange appears in sinister circumstances—until we cringe at the sight of it. An orange, against all expectations, becomes a forerunner of death.

That's power. Coppola has invested an object with meaning that goes beyond the literal, beyond its physical value, its taste, its smell, its weight and texture in your hand. And he does this through associative repetition.

It isn't a mystical process. Pavlov rings a bell and serves a dish of food—and before long the dog knows the meaning of the sound, saliva oozing along its chops. When you bring two things together in a meaningful sequence, you can accomplish more than Eliot's objective correlative. In fiction and nonfiction, especially when you're not relying on simple A-to-Z plotting, associative repetition is key to narrative cohesion and can also be used as a tool for thematic and character development.

I. Objects

Charles Baxter, in his essay collection *Burning Down the House*, gives this trick a name—rhyming action—and when discussing it he uses the example of Nabokov's Lolita. The bubble gum she is always snapping and popping between half-formed sentences at the beginning of the novel "rhymes" with the bubble of blood that rises from Clare Quilty's mouth at the end of the novel. The visual representation of her innocence has been consumed by Quilty. "The gum is still echoing there, but now it's grown up, gone through adolescence, and become bloody," Baxter writes.

You see the same trick in Dumbo's magic feather, in the coin in Cormac McCarthy's *No Country for Old Men,* in the urinal puck in Brady Udall's *The Miracle Life of Edgar Mint.* Tim O'Brien's *The Things They Carried* is another fitting example. How do most war stories open? With shrapnel whizzing by, blood splattering. Not O'Brien's. He places Lt. Jimmy Cross at the bottom of a foxhole, where, instead of ducking bullets, he's reading letters from a girl named Martha. "They were not love letters, but Lieutenant Cross was hoping, so he kept them folded in plastic at the bottom of his rucksack. In the late afternoon, after a day's march, he would dig his foxhole, wash his hands under a canteen, unwrap the letters, hold them with the tips of his fingers, and spend the last hour of light pretending." There are photographs, too. And a pebble from the Jersey shoreline that Martha sends him by mail. Through them, we understand that Lt. Cross has his head in the clouds, not in the trenches.

Most stories are about transformation. The narrative arc is aligned with the emotional arc of a character. In *The Wizard of Oz,* Dorothy goes from dreamer (singing "Somewhere over the Rainbow") to realist ("There's no place like home," she says, clicking her ruby heels). Same goes for Lt. Cross. And we understand this through meaningful repetition. Again and again the letters and photos flutter through the story—and again and again we hear about the death of Ted Lavender, each time learning more about it—and we begin to understand their alignment, the purpose of the recurrence. Cross comes to believe, and maybe he's right, that Lavender died because of him. Because he was too lax with the men, wasn't

a soldier to them, a leader. "No more fantasies, he told himself."
He crouches at the bottom of his foxhole and burns the letters and
photos even as he realizes that "Lavender was dead. You couldn't
burn the blame."

II. Setting

Most people don't associate *Toy Story* with sadness and angst, and most
people don't think of oranges as symbols of imminent doom. Most
people think that kitchen tables are where families come together in
fellowship, but David Mamet, in his essay "The Rake: A Few Scenes
from My Childhood," invests the setting with a sinister quality:

> The table was not in the kitchen proper but in an area called
> the "nook," which held its claim to that small measure of
> charm by dint of a waist-high wall separating it from an adja-
> cent area known as the living room.
>
> All family meals were eaten in the nook. There was a din-
> ing room to the right, but, as in most rooms of that name at
> the time and in those surroundings, it was never used.
>
> The round table was of wrought iron and topped with
> glass; it was noteworthy for that glass, for it was more than
> once and rather more than several times, I am inclined to
> think, that my stepfather would grow so angry as to bring
> some object down on the glass top, shattering it, thus giving
> us to know how we had forced him out of control.
>
> And it seems that most times when he would shatter the
> table, as often as that might have been, he would cut some por-
> tion of himself on the glass, or that he or his wife, our mother,
> would cut their hands on picking up the glass afterward, and
> that we children were to understand, and did understand, that
> these wounds were our fault.
>
> So the table was associated in our minds with the notion of
> blood.

The violence at the table continues. Mamet's sister joins the high school drama society and lands the starring role in a play. On opening night, she feels too nervous to eat. Her parents demand she finish her meal, and when she refuses, her mother calmly leaves the table, picks up the phone, calls the school, and tells them that her daughter will not be attending the performance that night.

By the end of the essay, after so much hate, so much abuse, we can hardly bear the thought of dragging up a chair and joining this family for a meal. In the final scene, that's exactly what Mamet forces us to do. After he and his sister get into a fight while raking the lawn—a fight that results in Mamet accidentally slicing his sister's lip with a rake—their mother asks them what happened:

> Neither of us—myself out of guilt, of course, and my sister out of a desire to avert the terrible punishment she knew I would receive—would say what occurred.
>
> My mother pressed us, and neither of us would answer. She said that until one or the other answered, we would not go to the hospital, and so the family sat down to dinner, where my sister clutched a napkin to her face and the blood soaked the napkin and ran down onto her food, which she had to eat; and I also ate my food, and we cleared the table and went to the hospital.

Charlotte Perkins Gilman does something similar with yellow wallpaper. And Zora Neale Hurston with porches as places where stories are told and gossip is traded, with a certain pear tree (where a "dust-bearing bee sink[s] into the sanctum of a bloom") as the ideal of love that no man she meets can live up to.

Alice Munro is the queen of rhyming action, which has for her an added purpose: the rhymes help to stabilize the digressive, nonchronological structure of many of her stories. Read "Miles City, Montana," and consider the way water—the reservoir that drowns the boy, the flood that threatens the farm, the swimming pool that nearly kills the narrator's daughter—creates a sense of foreboding, foreshadowing, and causality in a story that might otherwise seem free-associative in its movement and purpose.

III. Manner of Speech

Raymond Carver, in his essay "On Writing," notes that "it's possible, in a poem or a short story, to write about commonplace things and objects using commonplace but precise language, and to endow those things—a chair, a window curtain, a fork, a stone, a woman's earring—with immense, even startling power." Carver does just that in "Menudo" with a pile of leaves—and in "Collectors" with a vacuum cleaner—and in "Fat" with fingers. But he also pulls off the trick with language. Take his essay "My Father's Life," for instance. From the very first line, names matter:

> My dad's name was Clevie Raymond Carver. His family called
> him Raymond and his friends called him C. R. I was named
> Raymond Clevie Carver, Jr. I hated the "Junior" part. When
> I was little my dad called me Frog, which was okay. But later,
> like everybody else in the family, he began calling me Junior.
> He went on calling me this until I was thirteen or fourteen and
> announced that I wouldn't answer to that name any longer.
> So he began calling me Doc. From then until his death, on
> June 17, 1967, he called me Doc, or else Son.

Carver struggles, over the next few pages, to understand his father, their pained, difficult relationship. It is only after his father dies that Carver feels love for him, a prideful connection, and we learn about this through their names:

> After the service at the funeral home, after we had moved
> outside, a woman I didn't know came over to me and said,

"He's happier where he is now." I stared at this woman until she moved away. I still remember the little knob of a hat she was wearing. Then one of my dad's cousins—I didn't know the man's name—reached out and took my hand. "We all miss him," he said, and I knew he wasn't saying it just to be polite.

I began to weep for the first time since receiving the news. I hadn't been able to before. I hadn't had the time, for one thing. Now, suddenly, I couldn't stop. I held my wife and wept while she said and did what she could do to comfort me there in the middle of that summer afternoon.

I listened to people say consoling things to my mother, and I was glad that my dad's family had turned up, had come to where he was. I thought I'd remember everything that was said and done that day and maybe find a way to tell it sometime. But I didn't. I forgot it all, or nearly. What I do remember is that I heard our name used a lot that afternoon, my dad's name and mine. But I knew they were talking about my dad. *Raymond,* these people kept saying in their beautiful voices out of my childhood. *Raymond.*

He hears that name—Raymond, Raymond—and it echoes the opener and reveals how much he has changed, how he has come to feel closer to his father in part because they share the same failings. He is burdened by the name, yes, but he has also earned it.

It's useful to think of this technique as akin to a chorus in a song, where the repetition of certain lyrics earns them meaning and makes them more than just pretty sounds. The first time Johnny Cash sings, "I will let you down / I will make you hurt" in his cover of "Hurt" by Nine Inch Nails, for example, we're tapping our feet, but by the end of the song we've gone still, our eyes damp, our mouths pinched.

When I begin a story, I don't lay out on the desk of my mind an asthma inhaler, the color blue, a unicorn key chain, and AC/DC's

"Back in Black," then clap my hands together and say, "Let's get juggling!" Instead, every day when I sit down to write, I read what I have already written—from the first page of my short story or essay or from the beginning of a chapter of my novel. After reading and rereading my work, certain objects or settings begin to sizzle and glow—and eventually a grid of electricity emerges, a constellation that aligns the disparate parts.

The opening scene of my story "Refresh, Refresh," which concerns an Oregon town emptied of its men when a National Guard unit is activated, finds two boys boxing in a backyard ring made out of a garden hose laid tip to tip. I realized—not right away, but over time—that this backyard ring mildly resembled a meteor crater that appears in a subsequent scene. And that this crater resembled the cavity from a mortar blast. The backyard fights continue throughout the story, like a kind of chorus—and as their volume grows more severe I consciously made their connection to the crater (and to the war overseas) more obvious, the grass smearing away beneath their sneakers, the cinders kicked away until a shallow depression forms that "looks a lot like scabbed flesh." Blood is spilled in the backyard—and I knew that blood had to spill at the edge of the crater.

A meteor falls to the earth and a sled bombs down a steep hill and a peregrine falcon dives to claw a chipmunk and the war descends and seizes these men. Breath fogs the air and smoke rises from cigarettes and exhaust spews from tailpipes as if everything, everyone were lit from within. Even the phrase "Refresh, Refresh" is repeated, at first to reference email, but it has occurred to more than a few readers that, by the end of the story, the words also refer to the generational refreshment of troops, the inheritance of violence.

I'm talking about more than symbolism here—I'm talking about aligning the narrative, creating a sense of structural and thematic cohesion, satisfying the emotional arcs of characters. So the tropes are realized and what begins as tooth-and-claw instinct becomes deliberate, methodical carpentry.

I've offered many examples, some of them obvious, some of them subtle. I would encourage subtlety. Nabokov's bubble gum or Munro's water over Dumbo's magic feather. The pattern doesn't have to announce itself with a bullhorn to work. As the poet knows, and as Baxter writes, "Rhymes are often most telling when they are barely heard, when they are registered but not exactly noticed. . . . I think it's often more effective if the echo effects, the rhyming action, are allowed to happen without the reader being quite aware of them."

Toy Story is just another movie. An orange is just another fruit. The corner of Eighty-Sixth and Lexington is just another intersection. A table is just a place to have dinner. Until they're tossed into the air—and with each pass through the juggler's hands they gain power and meaning.

Home Improvement
Revision as Renovation

The Realtor said, "It's got good bones." That's what people say about ugly houses—and this was an ugly house. No one had done a thing to it since 1965, the year it was built. Every inch of the place was plastered with flocked or floral-patterned wallpaper, even the insides of the cabinets. All the light fixtures were white orbs collared by thin brass rings. The outside of the oven grew as hot as the inside. The master bedroom had curtains that matched its shaggy carpet that resembled in its color nothing so much as mint-green gum. The roof was rotten and sagging. The furnace and gutters were rusted out.

But my wife and I walked through the backyard, a good quarter acre of rich grass bordered by shade plants and mature ash trees whose branches came together overhead like a cathedral's roof. And we stood before the river-rock fireplaces and sat on the three-season porch and laid our hands flat along the walls and smiled as you would when rubbing a belly ripe with pregnancy. And bought the place.

This was April of 2008, and we were shoving books into boxes, packing up the moving truck, when the phone rang with good news: I had sold my novel *The Wilding*. My editor at Graywolf Press, Fiona McCrae, said how excited she was about the manuscript, but wondered if I might be amenable to some changes. "Of course," I said. What did she have in mind? "How about let's start with the point of view?" she said. "Might we shift it from first to third? And in doing so, with the freedom afforded to the characters, perhaps we could add some plotlines that threaded together?" The book had good bones, in other words, but it needed some renovation.

Fiona has a British accent and somehow this makes everything she says sound reasonable. So I said, "Sure, no problem"—and I meant it. I recognized the narrative as less of a novel and more of an extended short story, a "shnovel." Here was the architectural solution, a new blueprint delivered from contractor to carpenter. I felt fired-up, ready to flip open my toolbox and get to work. It wasn't until later, when I printed the manuscript and began to riffle through its pages, that I shuddered at the job ahead of me.

I'm no stranger to starting over. I wrote four failed novels before selling *The Wilding*. They were not a waste of time, not at all. I learned from them the humility that comes from watching something you've spent years working on turn to dust in your hands. And I discovered—by dissecting their cold carcasses—the many ways I might rob their organs and bones, their images and characters and settings and metaphors, and rearrange them, reimagine them, as short stories.

"Refresh, Refresh" is a good example. For my graduate thesis I wrote a (wretched) novel called *King of the Wild Frontier* (panned by students, faculty, agents, and editors alike). The fight scenes that appear in "Refresh, Refresh" are almost directly lifted from it, though their context couldn't be more different. Neither could the early and late drafts of the short story. Originally, "Refresh, Refresh" was supernatural—my agent, Katherine Fausset, helped me transform it into scorched-earth realism. Originally it was forty pages—and Nat Rich at the *Paris Review* helped me winnow it down to eighteen. Originally the grandfather played a much larger role, and his subplot involved an amputated foot preserved in a bucket of formaldehyde—he ended up getting his own story, "The Killing" (which also recycles a number of scenes from *King of the Wild Frontier*). I could go on about the axed weight-lifting scenes, the three boys that became two, the brain-damaged vet, Floyd, who every night set up his karaoke machine outside the Dairy Queen and served as a kind of Greek chorus. Gone.

So much of revision, I've discovered, is about coming to terms with that word: *gone.* Letting things go. When revising, the beginning writer spends hours consulting the thesaurus, replacing a period with a semicolon, cutting adjectives, adding a few descriptive sentences—whereas the professional writer mercilessly lops off limbs, rips out innards like party streamers, drains away gallons of blood, and then calls down the lightning to bring the body back to life.

My editor at *Esquire,* Tyler Cabot, helped me figure this out. He once commissioned me to write a story about April 20, a cursed day on the calendar known for being, among other things, the proximate date of Hitler's birthday, the Oklahoma City bombing, the Waco siege, the Columbine shootings, the Deepwater Horizon oil disaster. He wanted me to write a story that incorporated the larger mythology and that also read like today's news, since it would hit magazine racks around that same date. I had two weeks. And for two weeks, all I did was hammer. I would shoot him a draft and he would say things like "I dig this dialogue exchange. Lose the rest," or "Not ballsy enough," or "This is kind of sucking. Start over." At one point, as we neared the deadline, he offered a kill fee—and then he called back an hour later and said, "Come on, man. You can do this. One more draft." One more draft made ten drafts. And the tenth draft sold. I wrote over one hundred pages for the thirteen that were published.

Revision doesn't come easy. That's why I used to resist it. When I received comments on my work, my eyes skimmed over the criticism and homed in on the compliments. That's no way to be. Let me tell you something: if you've got the angel in one ear, whispering kind things, and the devil in the other, hissing about how badly you stink, listen to the devil. The devil drives revision.

You've got to write every day as if you were clocking in for a job. Or if not every day, then damn near it. If you're not disciplined in your production—if you're writing only when the mood strikes or when a deadline looms—then naturally you'll be more protective of your work, so that when it comes time to cut, your saw will tremble with hesitation. But if you're producing reams of pages, you'll be less resistant to revision, because you know it won't be long before another load of timber comes down the road.

I discovered this in grad school, when writing became a full-time job and when critiques became sharp-toothed, long-nailed. One time a professor handed me back a manuscript with every single page slashed through with an enormous black *X*. There were no comments except a single word scrawled over the title: *Don't*. When I later spoke to the professor, I pushed him further, asking what he meant, exactly, by "Don't." Don't what? Don't bother? Was the story no good? No, he said. That wasn't it. He liked the story—"Just *don't* write it that way." His advice served as an eraser. I pretended the original document no longer existed, and when I began another draft, it filled up a clean white screen unchained by the rusted-out sentences written previously.

Not much has changed. Helen Atsma, my editor at Grand Central Publishing, might as well have written "Don't" when editing my novels *Red Moon* and *The Dead Lands*. Subplots and characters needed to go. The third act was confusing and unsatisfactory and needed to be completely reimagined. I used the word *growl* too often. That kind of thing. I highlighted a dozen pages here, a hundred pages there, hit DELETE, and started over.

I have thrown away thousands of pages—and sometimes you need to do that; sometimes you have to start over. But sometimes you don't. Sometimes your story needs some serious renovation—the walls are full of mold, the roof is leaking—and sometimes it simply needs some cosmetic work, a little paint splashed on the walls.

I've discovered that revision is far less intense and traumatic when I begin a story with its end in mind. I used to be an organic writer who had no game plan, who followed my tooth-and-claw instinct, who considered writing an act of discovery. I let the garden grow and returned to it later to trim back the tangles, rip out the weeds. Dan Chaon—the author of such dynamite story collections as *Among the Missing*—is such a writer. For every fifteen-page short story he produces more than a hundred pages. His stories "Big Me" and "The Bees" went through so many drafts that "I would have probably been better off writing a novel," he says. Sometimes he lays the pages down on the floor and wanders among them, rearranging them, isolating some scenes, crumpling up others and tossing them aside, until finally he decides what the story is *about* and returns to his desk to realize the piece in a shorter form.

On the other end of the spectrum is the LEGO writer. She has her exact design in mind and snaps each piece into place and pleasures in how tidily everything comes together. I've tried this, too, and though it might work for some, for me, it makes the act of writing feel lifeless, boring.

I now fall somewhere between these two categories. I know my ending—maybe not everything about it, but generally where things will close, what will happen—and I know one or two scenes that occur in the middle. In aiming for them, I take far fewer wrong turns.

I used to consider editing something you did once a story was completed. I now begin each day by reading what I have already written. If it's a short story, I mean from the first line forward. If it's a novel, I mean from the start of the chapter I'm working on. I sometimes spend hours editing before I shift to an imaginative mode and begin to punch out new material. So I'm essentially in a constant state of revision, and by the time I finish the story, I might have edited it two dozen times, turning it over and over in my hands, sanding it until it's free of slivers.

Faulkner said, Kill your darlings, and in that tradition I created a Cemetery folder. (No doubt you are less morbid than I am, so

feel free to call yours The Compost Heap—the idea is the same.) In
it I have files—tombstones, I call them—with titles like "Images"
or "Metaphors" or "Characters" or "Dialogue." Into these I dump
and bury anything excised from a story. For some reason, having
a cemetery makes it easier to cut, to kill. Because I know the writing isn't lost—it has a place—and I can always return to the freshly
shoveled grave and perform a voodoo ceremony.

It took me a year to rewrite The Wilding, to move from first to
third person, to free up those characters and braid together their
stories. And when I handed it in to Fiona in March of 2009, she
said—again, in her British accent—"Fantastic. Exactly what we
wanted. Now would you mind cutting several of these subplots?
And fixing these plot holes? And while we're at it, how about let's
rethink the ending?" And, and, and.

And then I got back to work.

I was hammering at the keyboard all week, and hammering at
my house all weekend. I ripped out the carpeting, wrenched out the
thousands of tacks and staples to reveal gleaming hardwood. I scored
the wallpaper and sprayed it with hot, soapy water and scraped—and
scraped—and scraped away damp bits of paper, leaving the drywall
beneath pitted. So I mudded and sanded and textured and painted.
I tossed out the oven. I tossed out the curtains. I unscrewed the
cracked, yellowing outlets and light switches and replaced them
with white plates and once shocked myself so badly that my thumb-
nail bled and turned black. I pulled out the brass and shoved in
wrought-iron light fixtures. We had a new roof thrown on, new gutters hung.

After a few months, our Realtor stopped by to check on us. He
shook my hand—a hand yellowed with calluses and crosshatched
with scrapes, colored with bruises. He hardly recognized the house
he had sold us, just as I hardly recognized my novel as it moved from
first to final draft. "You've been working hard," he said, and I said,
"Yes."

Go the Distance

Many years ago, I took a break from my novel to write a short story called "In the Rough." My voice was used to wide-open spaces and didn't want to be corralled, so the sentences kept galloping forward, the scenes piling up, until the story was anything but short, a thirty-four-page beast with long claws and dangling genitals. I knew I was in trouble. Literary magazines generally aren't fond of anything that clocks in over eighteen pages. I couldn't figure out how to make it any slimmer, but I believed in the story, so I sent it off to the races. It wasn't long before the rejections came pouring in.

If I'm one thing, it's bullheaded. I once drank a bucket of hot-wing sauce to win a bet. I've stacked enough metal on the bench press to burst capillaries in my eyes. My wife is five years older than me—and out-of-my-league beautiful—but that didn't stop me, at the age of nineteen, from saying, "How you doing?" And in undergrad and graduate workshops, many students were more talented than I was, but I kept hammering long after they hung up their tools.

This is a lesson I learned from Rocky Balboa. I know some of you probably think it's decidedly unhip to be a fan of the Sylvester Stallone character all these years—and sequels—after the original movie came out, but I don't care. The original Rocky, the scrappy southpaw who lives in a filthy apartment and dreams of a better life, who rises early and falls asleep late, who wants only respect and who everybody thinks is a bum, has something to teach every writer trying to break into the business.

A framed poster of a black-eyed Stallone hangs above my desk. The blaring trumpets of the *Rocky* theme song sound every time my cell phone rings. He hovers over my shoulder like a ghost, whispering in my ear, "You stop this fight, I'll kill ya." And he was with me in grad school, when I lived in my own filthy apartment, when I woke up early to hit the keyboard and fell asleep late with a book in my hand, when I dreamed big, and when I created in Excel an elaborate tier system for submission.

Each tier consisted of ten or twenty literary magazines. In the top tier, you could find the *New Yorker,* the *Atlantic, Esquire,* the *Paris Review,* publications I would kill to get into, publications I really had no business submitting to in the first place. And then there was the second tier, the third tier, the fourth. I was, and still am, a voracious reader of journals, so I had done my homework and I knew whose door I wanted to kick down.

I would begin by sending five copies of one story to the top tier. For every rejection I received, I would send off five more copies to the second tier. For every second-tier rejection, five more copies went to the third tier. You can guess the rest of the formula. Luckily I'm a good bookkeeper, because I would sometimes have forty copies of the same manuscript circulating. Mind you, I don't do this anymore, but at the time, feeling like such a nobody and knowing how ugly the odds were, I took a David and Goliath approach to submission. The tier system was my stone in a sling.

You won't be surprised to hear that whole forests have been pulped to print the rejection letters sent my way. The mailman would deliver two or three to me each day. Mostly they were form rejections, but every now and then an editor would scribble a personal message like "Really enjoyed this, but the ending didn't work," or "Excellent imagery, but less blood next time, please." C. Michael Curtis, the esteemed fiction editor at the *Atlantic,* received way, way too many crappy manuscripts from me, and, bless his heart, he always wrote back. "Unrepentantly artificial," one read.

I wasn't offended. I was inspired. I would tape his—and so many other editorial remarks—to the wall near my desk. The wall of shame, I called it. Everybody thought I was a bum, like Rocky, or so I thought. And every morning, when I woke up to hammer, I would stand there, coffee mug hot in my hand. My thoughts, staring at their comments, were somewhere between I'm going to get you, and I'd better do better.

I know, I know: the editor-writer relationship should not be thought of as adversarial. Editors are there to discover and culture writers, to coach them along. But that's just the way my mind works: everybody is in the ring with me. When I was a new dad, I couldn't even go on a walk without eyeing somebody else's stroller and thinking, My kid's cuter than yours.

So when I was first starting out, I liked to think of editors as all looking like Burgess Meredith playing coach Mickey Goldmill—wearing ill-fitting gray sweatsuits, whistles dangling around their necks. And I liked to think of myself working the speed bag or jumping rope until my heels blistered over. "Is that all you've got?" they screamed. "Work harder, you wuss!" I was, like any struggling athlete, full of resentment and respect. I wanted to do better to impress them, yes, but also to demonstrate something to myself. I wanted to go the distance.

It's like Rocky says: "I was nobody. But that don't matter either, you know? 'Cause I was thinking, it really don't matter if I lose this fight. It really don't matter if this guy opens my head, either. 'Cause all I wanna do is go the distance. Nobody's ever gone the distance with Creed, and if I can go that distance, you see, and that bell rings and I'm still standing, I'm gonna know for the first time in my life, see, that I weren't just another bum from the neighborhood." So every day I would spend eight hours at the keyboard—and every week I would trek to the post office weighed down by stacks of manila envelopes.

You know how many rejections "In the Rough" racked up? Thirty-nine. All that time, I kept swinging, and just when I was about to give up, the phone rang. It was the editor of the *Antioch Review,* a journal with bigger muscles than almost all those who had rejected the story. A few months after publication, Salman Rushdie listed "In the Rough" as one of the "100 Distinguished Stories" in *Best American Short Stories 2008.*

This isn't supposed to be self-congratulatory—this is supposed to be a rallying cry. You've got to keep swinging, no matter how painful the fight. I have a friend from grad school who gave up on an extraordinary story after a single rejection; I'm not surprised, but I'm sorry to report that he's no longer writing. Others aren't quite so sensitive, but after five rejections, seven, ten, they're usually ready to throw in the towel. Every time an editor says no it's like a fist to the face. But you've got to see through the blood— you've got to keep breathing raggedly through those broken ribs— you've got to remember the thirty-ninth rejection.

Of course, I've written ten times as many stories as I've published. There isn't always a happy ending to submitting widely, stubbornly. Sometimes the rejections pile up for good reason. The story lacks heart. The dialogue stinks. The ending is actually the beginning. Your narrator is a talking pony. With cancer. Whatever.

But you already know this. You know how hard it is to make a story right. You know about the long, painful apprenticeship that requires you to read and write with the same discipline and heart that make Rocky slam his fists into slabs of frozen meat, jog furiously up the art museum stairs, climb a mountain in knee-deep snow with a log balanced on his back.

After you spend those countless hours pushing sentences around, after you polish a story until it glows, nobody is going to approach you on the street and seize your hand and say, "Congratulations! You did it!" There's more work to be done. The same stubborn mind-set that informs your craft must inform the often frustrating, sometimes humiliating work of submission (such an apt word, no?). And you need to know that breaking into magazines is about talent, yes, but also doggedness.

When submitting your work, know the odds. Look at a magazine like *Glimmer Train*. Every year it receives some forty thousand submissions—of which it publishes about forty. Yeah. That means no matter how badass your story is, it's probably going to get rejected. Take the hit. Smile through your mouth guard. Retreat to your corner. Spit into a bucket. Say a few Hail Marys. Then get back in the fight.

And realize how curious and complicated the editorial decision-making process is. I've seen an editor walk into a room stacked high with submissions, sigh with regret, and say, "Clear them out," simply because the next two issues were full. Or maybe the editor ate a bad burrito that makes everything he reads that day seem awful. Or maybe the journal already accepted a story about a tap-dancing dwarf and a magic bowie knife. Or maybe you pissed off one of the interns at a writing conference and they sent your story straight to recycling. Or, or, or. There are so many reasons that rejections might appear in your in box. Sometimes it's because the story isn't strong enough, but sometimes it isn't. Regardless, you must develop around your heart a callus the size of a speed bag.

Thirty-nine rejections. Remember that the next time you're feeling low at the keyboard or thumbing open a letter addressed "Dear Writer." And then pop the *Rocky* sound track into your stereo, tape your knuckles and wrists, ram your hands into gloves, and step into that ring ready to last twelve rounds against Apollo Creed. Go the distance.

Acknowledgments

Many of these essays began as lectures delivered at the Tin House Summer Writers' Workshop and the low-residency MFA program at Pacific University. Thanks to Rob Spillman, Lance Cleland, and Shelley Washburn for getting me up onstage, and thanks to the students for enduring my fire and brimstone.

These lectures then became essays, and Kevin Larimer edited and published versions of them in *Poets & Writers* magazine. This book wouldn't exist without his encouragement over the years. Smaller portions of a few of these essays (sometimes a paragraph, sometimes a page) also appeared in *Esquire,* the *Washington Post,* the *LA Times,* and *Glimmer Train* (thanks to Linda Swanson-Davies). And the AWP *Writer's Chronicle* published the essay on set pieces under the title "The Indelible Image: Moments Make Movies, Moments Make Stories." My pal Aaron Gwyn and I worked together on "Techniques of Violence" and copublished it in *Poets & Writers.* I've expanded the essay considerably since, but I'm grateful for his contributions to it and for his permission to include it here.

Thanks, as always, to the pack at Graywolf Press for their bigheartedness and friendship, their editorial and marketing savvy. Jeff Shotts and Steve Woodward were especially helpful in polishing and shaping this book.

Thanks to Katherine Fausset, my agent, and Stuart Waterman,

her assistant, for supporting the project and fussing over paperwork that needed to be fussed over.

And finally, thanks to my wife, Lisa, for her encouragement, tolerance, and love.

BENJAMIN PERCY is a novelist, comics writer, and screenwriter. He is the author of the novels *The Dead Lands, Red Moon,* and *The Wilding,* as well as two short-fiction collections, *Refresh, Refresh* and *The Language of Elk.* His fiction and nonfiction have been aired on NPR, performed at Symphony Space, and published in *Esquire* (where he is a contributing editor), *GQ, Time,* the *Wall Street Journal, Men's Journal, Ploughshares,* the *Paris Review, Tin House, Glimmer Train,* and *McSweeney's.* His honors include an NEA Literature Fellowship, a Whiting Award, two Pushcart Prizes, the Plimpton Prize, and inclusion in *The Best American Short Stories, The Best American Comics,* and *100 Years of the Best American Short Stories.* He writes the Green Arrow and Teen Titans series for DC Comics. Learn more about him at www.benjaminpercy.com.

The text of *Thrill Me* is set in FF Clifford Nine. Book design by Ann Sudmeier. Composition by Bookmobile Design & Digital Publisher Services, Minneapolis, Minnesota. Manufactured by Versa Press on acid-free, 30 percent postconsumer wastepaper.